Transform Your Travel Business

UNLOCK THE SECRETS TO EXPLOSIVE GROWTH AND SALES WITH MARKETING, MINDSET, AND MOTIVATION

Victoria R. Henley
MBA, CTA, VTA

Dedication

To all my family, thank you for your support.
Live your best life ever, with GrAtitude.

Table of Contents

———————————— • ————————————

"I believe the key to success is maintaining a positive mindset and embracing every opportunity that comes your way."

—Michele Voss,
Founder and CEO of OutOfOffice.com

Should Selling Travel Really Be This Hard?

At 52, Liz thought she'd found her second calling when she launched her home-based travel agency focused on group travel experiences. After years of corporate life, she was eager to build something of her own. But now, a year in, her business feels like a constant uphill battle. Each week starts with early mornings spent cold emailing potential clients and organizations, trying to pitch group trips to various communities. By mid-morning, she's scouring social media, hoping to catch someone's attention with her posts about curated group adventures, but engagement is low, and conversions even lower. Her afternoons are filled with phone calls, follow-ups, and crafting proposals, but many of her leads turn out to be hesitant or simply uninterested. Group travel was becoming more challenging for her to sell. She feels people are more cautious with their spending. She hears from some clients that they are hesitant to commit to group trips due to concerns over flexibility and traveler safety and that securing bookings is laborious. Fast forward to Friday. Liz is emotionally drained and keeps returning to why her efforts haven't paid off. She has tried everything possible to make her travel business successful, from discounts and promotions to even pursuing small partnerships. Her struggle isn't from a lack of trying. Liz is simply overwhelmed by the challenges of a rapidly changing travel market.

At 45, Kattie wakes up every morning feeling a mix of dread and exhaustion. Her home-based travel agency, once her dream, has become a source of constant stress. She built a website, ran local newspaper ads, and posted on social media. Like Liz mentioned earlier, nothing works. The first thing she does in the morning is check her phone and emails, hoping for any small sign that her hard work might pay off. Instead, she finds an empty email inbox and no text or voicemail messages from prospects or clients. By 7 am, she's downstairs. She scrolls through her social media, crafting the perfect post to grab attention. It's a lonely process. Her follower count barely budges, and engagement is dismal. She spends an hour tweaking her website, ensuring it's up-to-date, but deep down, she knows it's not enough. By 9 am, Kattie attempts to call past clients, but only a few answer and the conversations are short. None are ready to book a trip. She, too, is overwhelmed, stuck in a cycle of effort that yields little return. Her struggle is caused by the overwhelming uncertainty of what to do next. She feels like she's sinking, unsure how to turn it around. She attempts to make follow-up calls to past clients, but few answer and none seem interested in booking. She wonders if she's doing something wrong or if the industry has changed too much for her to keep up. It's a harsh realization that the dream she once believed in is slipping through her fingers, leaving her feeling lost, defeated, and unsure how to turn things around.

At 38, Marc wakes up every weekday at 6 am. His optimistic energy becomes a heavy weight of his struggling home-based travel agency. His passion and focus have always been on luxury travel. Marc feels well-suited to catering to high-end clients who want flawless experiences. But despite his best efforts, sales remain stagnant. He spends his mornings cold-calling prospects, trying to land meetings with prospective luxury travelers, but the conversations often fizzle out. By mid-morning, he's updating his website, refining his marketing strategies, and sending follow-up emails, but with little return. Marc's afternoons are spent on social media, trying to break through the noise with curated content about exclusive destinations. He's learned the importance of digital marketing, but the competition is fierce, and getting noticed in a crowded luxury travel space feels impossible. The high expectations of potential clients mean they're picky and slow to commit, often ghosting him after promising leads. By Thursday, he's drained, questioning whether he's missing something crucial. He's tried everything- advertising, networking, influencer partnerships- but nothing seems to create the momentum he needs. He feels overwhelmed by the constant hustle and self-doubt, knowing his struggle isn't from a lack of effort. Today's travel industry is different- more competitive and fragmented, and Marc is struggling to adapt. He's unsure how to pivot, and every week feels like a repeat of the last.

You're Not Alone

Being an advisor, agency owner, and even a home-based entrepreneur makes it easy for travel professionals to feel overwhelmed and isolated, especially when sales, profits, and revenue seem stagnant or declining. You're not alone in facing these challenges. The travel industry has undergone significant transformations during the mid-2020s and is dynamic, from shifting customer expectations and the introduction of AI technology to new consumer protections and government policy changes. The rise of OTA's (online travel agencies), the increased demand for personalized experiences, and the impact of economic and political global events have all reshaped how the travel industry does business. As a result, it impacts and changes the way we, as travel professionals, must do business. Do you feel like you're constantly playing catch-up? Are you trying to adapt to these rapid changes while your competitors seem to thrive? There is hope. This book is a compilation of proven marketing strategies designed to help travel professionals succeed. These strategies will help you generate more leads and sales, leading to increased profit and streamlined operations for greater efficiency. The marketing strategies you'll find here are specifically designed for the evolving landscape of the travel industry. You are given the tools you need to stay competitive. It's time to take control of your business, revitalize your sales pipeline, and start seeing the growth you deserve. The marketing solutions are here, and your future success begins now!

The travel industry underwent significant changes from 2021 to 2024 and continues to be fluid, creating new challenges for travel professionals. Here are important ways the industry has changed in recent years:

Increased Competition from Online Travel Agencies (OTAs)

The rise of OTAs like Expedia, Booking.com, and Airbnb has made it easier for consumers to book travel directly. Traditional travel agencies have increased competition. It is often more difficult for smaller home-based travel professionals to stand out and secure bookings.

Changing Consumer Expectations

Travelers are interested in unique experiences. Rather than the standard packages, travelers now seek flexibility and customization. Today's travel professionals cater to a broader range of preferences, requiring more time for research and increased resources.

Impact of Global Events (Political, Pandemic, Economic Uncertainty)

The COVID-19 pandemic and subsequent political and economic disruptions have affected travel patterns. Travel demand has recovered. However, unpredictable events such as new travel restrictions, consumer advocacy, and global economic challenges create uncertainty. It is difficult for travel professionals to predict demand and manage operations effectively.

Technology Advancements and Digital Transformation

The shift to digital platforms and mobile services has forced travel agencies to adopt new technologies to stay competitive. From AI itinerary creation and booking software to marketing automation, travel professionals must now invest in technology education and technology solutions, which adds complexity and cost to their operations.

Changing Travel Trends (Bleisure, Remote Work, Eco-Tourism)

The rise and fall of remote work have led to changing customer demands. Travel professionals must adapt to evolving trends, such as travelers combining business and leisure travel or offering eco-tourism services and other hybrid travel needs.

A Reason for Hope

Despite these challenges, there are several reasons for optimism. These challenges present new opportunities for travel professionals. Which digital tools are you embracing? Are you interested in or have you developed a passion for a niche market different from your current expertise? Leveraging personalized services can set travel professionals apart. The marketing strategies outlined in this book will equip you with the skills to adapt to these changes, reconnect with customers, and thrive in the evolving travel landscape. Success is achievable with the right marketing strategies in place.

Time To Break The Cycle

The travel industry has always been dynamic, but it has become increasingly complex and fast-moving in the past few years. As a travel agency owner, you're probably feeling the pressure from changing consumer expectations, heightened competition, and the rapid pace of technological advancements. It's easy to think that the solution requires drastic changes, but the truth is, it's not about reinventing the wheel. You need more thoughtful, efficient strategies to thrive without overhauling everything you've built.

Let's face it, you're already juggling multiple responsibilities as a business owner and travel advisor. Between managing customer relationships, handling operations, keeping track of bookings, and trying to stay on top of marketing, it can feel like there's no time to think about long-term growth strategies. You might not have the luxury (and do not need) to revamp your business entirely, but you can make small, incremental changes that will deliver significant results. The marketing strategies outlined in this book are compiled to help you do exactly that: work smarter, not harder.

Rather than adding more tasks, you will receive actionable recommendations on streamlining your current processes and focusing on the most impactful activities. You can maximize revenue and sales by organizing your time and resources more effectively without burning yourself out. It's about focusing on what matters most and eliminating activities that waste time or are not efficient. This approach will allow you to serve your clients and grow your business naturally, not forcefully.

The key to success in this new era of travel is not just about more work; it's about being disciplined and intentional with your efforts. You will learn how to organize and build structures that simplify your operations, freeing up time and resources to enhance customer experience. Ready to become more organized and proactive? With the right tools, you can manage your day-to-day operations and focus more on the bigger picture and long-term growth. This book isn't about reinventing your entire business but making it more efficient and profitable with marketing activities and efficient effort.

Moreover, the travel industry is shifting in ways that open up new opportunities, but these opportunities require a strategic approach. Consumer preferences have evolved, with many travelers seeking more personalized experiences, sustainable travel options, and flexibility. Instead of fighting these changes or feeling overwhelmed, you'll learn how to use them to your advantage. Beyond business operations, adjustments to customer service and marketing strategies, as found in this book, will help you align with these trends and stand out in a crowded marketplace.

It's time for a change, but not a radical one. The transformation we're aiming for is fine-tuning your approach to business. You don't need to overhaul everything you've worked hard to build. What you need is a shift in mindset, a move towards smarter work habits, and the discipline to implement the right systems. By laying this foundation, you'll create a business that survives and thrives in an evolving travel landscape. With the right strategies in place, you'll feel more in control, more organized, and more confident in the future of your travel agency.

You are not alone in this. Many travel agency owners face similar challenges, but with the right tools and the marketing strategies in this book, you'll be well on your way to creating a business poised for sustainable success.

So, fasten your seatbelt. Your travel business is about to soar!

———————•———————

CHAPTER TWO

"The key to success in the travel industry is passion, persistence, and the ability to see opportunities in every challenge."

—Renee Greenstein,
Founder of The Travel Concierge

Your Road to Success is Paved With Determination

Before we cruise ahead, we will dock here for a moment. Let's talk about determination. What does that word mean to you? Consider the importance of determination when running a business, especially a travel business. This book is about success and what it takes to earn it. So, I will address determination based on my experiences in the travel industry and corporate business world.

How determined are you? What is your willpower, resolve, and drive for business success? You must be determined to succeed. Determination is the driving force that keeps entrepreneurs in any business sector moving forward, even when faced with obstacles and setbacks. As travel advisors and travel agency owners, determination is essential. Without it, the challenges of building and growing a travel business can feel insurmountable, but with determination, every hurdle becomes an opportunity to learn and grow.

The path can sometimes feel uncertain in the travel industry, where market dynamics constantly change. But, here is the reality. The success principles are considered universal among many athletes, business professionals, celebrities- you name it. Unlocking the door to success in any endeavor requires consistency, dedication, and flexibility. Every business will face hurdles. It could be agonizing slow growth, concerning financial constraints, or debilitating moments of doubt. But these are the moments that will define your unique and successful journey.

Entrepreneurship requires us to step outside our comfort zones and embrace change. We must challenge ourselves to grow, evolve, and take risks to achieve true business success. It's easy to stay where things feel familiar and safe, but real growth happens when we push ourselves beyond the limits of what we know.

Max DePree, the legendary CEO of Herman Miller Furniture, told his board of directors, *"We cannot become what we want by remaining what we are,"* What a perfect sentiment that transcends the furniture business. In almost every aspect of life, a person cannot move forward without making a change. Mr. Depree's quote perfectly captures the idea of growing and evolving. If we keep doing things the way we've always done them, we'll stay stuck in the same place. That makes absolute sense. Success comes when we choose to evolve—when we let go of the habits, fears, or limitations that hold us back and open ourselves to new possibilities.

In business, this means trying new strategies, exploring uncharted territories, and facing challenges head-on. Every great entrepreneur has had to take that leap—leaving behind the comfort of the known to venture into the unknown.

The path to success isn't about staying comfortable. Part of your success is the ability to become a person capable of reaching the goals you set. It is worth repeating. Once again, as Max Depree artfully said, and it remains true, *"We cannot become what we want by remaining what we are..."* Becoming what we want personally and professionally requires that we must be willing to change, grow, and gather the courage to face the apprehension, self-doubt, and any other challenge that comes with taking that next step (no, leap!) forward.

You got this. Now, do it!

Remember, business success results from consistency, dedication, flexibility, and an unshakable resolve to achieve your goals. No matter the industry, including our beloved travel industry, the road to success is paved with effort, persistence, and the ability to rise above challenges.

You are capable of overcoming these challenges. You are ready to rise above. The travel business you're building, whether you're just starting or amid incredible growth, has the potential to become the foundation for the life you truly deserve. You didn't get into the travel business to get a discount on vacations! Because as you have already discovered, it doesn't automatically happen that way. So, stay focused. Stay committed. The hard work you put in today is what will shape your tomorrow. The future of your travel business and building a long list of satisfied clients is yours to create.

You have already made the brave choice to jump into the travel industry. That takes guts, so be proud. You dream of building a travel business that helps people create unforgettable experiences. That is endearing. And while you want to see everyone's travel dreams come true, you are in business. You must think like a businessperson. The number one unwritten rule in business: if it doesn't make money, it doesn't make sense. Unless you are a self-sustaining financial backer of your travel business, you must earn a profit. Businesses can only remain in operation and grow if they generate profit. It's Accounting 101. It's that simple. Let me be clear: there are no shortcuts in the travel business. There are no quick fixes and no secret formulas that will make you an overnight success. You must be consistent and determined.

You've probably had enough of reading about or hearing rumors of a travel professional that sold over $400k in luxury cruises, and only top sellers receive exclusive invites to DM luncheons. Or, you invested hundreds or even thousands of dollars to be part of a host agency, only to feel that you did not receive the needed sales or support to be successful. And the customer leads, let's not get started with those! If you want to build a truly successful travel business, it's time to stop chasing easy wins and start building something real.

Make today your reset point. Your success journey begins today, and it's time to get serious. It's time to focus on what works. And what works isn't flashy. It's not about finding the perfect trick or hack to "sell travel" without effort. It's like saying, I want to run a marathon without training regularly. Your success in crossing the finish line will be much more difficult. What works is simple, consistent effort. It's about making smart choices, day after day, and sticking with it when things aren't going perfectly—because they won't.

You probably already know that success is built on a foundation of small decisions that, over time, add up to something bigger than you could ever imagine.

Every client you book. Every conversation you have. Every marketing strategy you test. Every late night spent refining your business plans. These are the building blocks of your future success. It's not glamorous, and it's not easy. But it's the only way forward. When you're in this business, you'll need to make thousands of small choices, each one shaping the future of your business.

Maybe you're sitting here thinking, *"I'm doing everything right. I'm putting in the effort. Why am I not seeing instant results?"* And I get it. We live in a world where we expect things to happen quickly, especially when we see others succeed. We wonder, what am I doing wrong? But remember, success isn't about a single "win." It's about being there consistently and building trust with your customers. It's about giving them value in the services you offer and how you serve them.

There's no shortcut to gaining that trust. There isn't one special email that will suddenly skyrocket your business. As you imagine, no social media post will bring in hundreds of clients overnight. It's a long game. And the sooner you accept that the sooner you'll realize that consistency is the key.

Now, consistency doesn't just mean doing the same thing every day. It means showing up with intent. Investing your energy into the right tasks will move the needle. Planning, evaluating, and adjusting. You need a strategy, and it needs to be a living thing. This business will evolve, and your strategies need to evolve with it. But you can't build that without a clear vision, discipline, and time.

Don't think of today as a "fantasy reset" where things suddenly click. Think of it as your opportunity to press the restart button to refine your processes, goals, and approach. To strip away anything that's not working and focus solely on what will move you closer to your vision.

So, ask yourself: Are you making an effort to truly understand your customers' needs? Are you constantly seeking ways to provide more value to them? Are you testing new ways of marketing and selling your services while being mindful of where your time and energy are best spent?

It's not about perfection. It is about progress. These are the small, daily actions that add up. There is no need to fall into the trap of chasing after overnight success. The reality is that those who embrace the daily work, those who make the tough decisions every day, will look back a year from now and be proud of how far they've come.

So, what does success look like for you? What is your vision of success? It should not be about working 24/7 and burning out in a year. Success is about setting realistic goals, consistently moving toward them, and adjusting along the way. The road will have its ups and downs but remember: the most successful business owners in travel aren't the ones who get inside information. They're the ones who kept showing up, made good decisions, and stayed the course, even when it wasn't easy.

Embrace this moment as your reset. Refine your goals. Get clear about your vision and start building with purpose. It's all about the small choices you make every day. Stick with it.

Be consistent and be patient. Stick with it. And most importantly—don't give up. Your dream of being a travel business leader is possible. But it's on you to make it happen.

Let's get to work.

———————— • ————————

CHAPTER THREE

"Success is about creating value, and in the travel industry,
that means offering unforgettable experiences."

—Gloria Guevara,
Former CEO of the World Travel & Tourism Council (WTTC)

Your Travel Sales Success Starts Now

Your Sales Success Starts Today

Right now, at this very moment, you have everything you need to thrive in the travel business. Understand that every challenge you face, every misstep, and every mistake is just part of the process. Make each one a stepping stone to success.

I know many of you have struggled. I struggled. Perhaps you tried hard and worked hard but ultimately felt like you were going nowhere. You might have felt like you were running in place. Then, you were confronted with disappointments. And, just maybe, you said to yourself, "This isn't for me. I'm not like the others. I do not have what it takes. Will I ever make it?"

I'm here to tell you that failure is a sign that you're on the right track. An odd thing to say or write? Not really. As a travel professional, every obstacle, failure, and disappointment is an opportunity to learn. We should never stop growing, educating ourselves, and refining our approach. That's why I'm sharing five common mistakes that so many of us travel professionals make and two that are less common but even more powerful. I know because I have made a few and observed others make them. These mistakes are the things that, when overcome, will set you on the path to success in selling your niche, interest, and passion, whether in group travel, women's wellness getaways, or even multi-generational luxury vacations.

Common Mistake #1: Chasing Every Lead

One of the biggest mistakes many travel professionals, particularly new advisors, make is chasing every lead that comes their way. It's tempting, I get it. You see a lead and think, "This could be the one! I can't let it slip by!" But here's the truth: not every lead is a good fit for you, and not every client will value your expertise. Do not risk losing focus and spreading yourself too thin by saying "yes" to everyone.

Solution: Narrow your niche and start specializing. Whether it's group travel, women's wellness retreats, or luxury vacations, find your sweet spot and become known for that. You can attract the type of business that truly resonates with you when you specialize. Of course, specializations build trust with clients and recognize that you are an expert in your field. As a result, you can attract the type of business that truly resonates with you.

Common Mistake #2: Undervaluing Your Services

Another mistake I see often is undervaluing yourself. When you're new to the business, you might feel pressured to offer discounts or low prices to compete. Short-term clients may result from offering low-cost services, but it doesn't create long-term loyalty. More importantly, it doesn't reflect the actual value of your efforts, expertise and knowledge.

Solution: Know your worth and charge accordingly. Your clients aren't just paying for a vacation—they're paying for your guidance, experience, and ability to craft seamless, personalized travel experiences. When you stop undervaluing yourself, you'll attract clients willing to invest in your travel experiences and other products because they respect your expertise.

 ## Common Mistake #3: Focusing Too Much on the Sale

Many travel advisors make the mistake of focusing solely on the sale—pushing for the booking, closing the deal, and moving on to the next client. But here's the thing: sales are essential, but building relationships will keep your business thriving in the long term.

Solution: Shift your focus to building genuine relationships with your clients. Make your interactions about the experience, not just the booking. Ask questions, get to know your clients' desires and pain points, and ensure you create the best possible experience. When you focus on relationships first, sales will follow naturally.

Common Mistake #4: Neglecting Marketing and Branding

It's easy to get caught up in the day-to-day operations of booking travel and forget about the importance of marketing and branding. If your potential clients don't know who you are, how can they trust you to book their dream vacations? You'll struggle to stand out without a strong online presence or clear marketing strategy.

Solution: Invest time in building your brand. Whether through social media, email newsletters, or a user-friendly website, ensure your marketing efforts are aligned with your target audience. Show them your expertise and unique value! People want to do business with someone they connect with and who stands out professionally.

🖐️ Common Mistake #5: Trying to Do It All Alone

When you start your travel business, wearing many hats is natural. In many cases, it is almost a requirement for survival initially. You're the marketer, the salesperson, the bookkeeper, and the customer service representative. But here's the truth: doing it alone is a surefire way to burn out. You can't grow your business to its fullest potential if you constantly juggle every task.

Solution: Delegate. Whether hiring a virtual assistant, working with a marketing expert, or partnering with logistics suppliers and vendors, don't be afraid to lean on others. As you grow, remember that you can't do it all—and that's perfectly okay. It's necessary for success.

Now, let's look at two less common mistakes that might not be as obvious but are critical to your success:

🖐️ Uncommon Mistake #1: Fearing Failure

As travel professionals, we often fear making mistakes because we ask clients to trust our expertise and use their hard earn money to pay for a trip and experience. This can cause a big miscalculation. We may fear losing a client or failing to deliver the perfect vacation.

Solution: The secret is understanding that failure is part of success. If you never fail, you will never learn. You can't avoid mistakes. Appreciate the opportunity to embrace and learn from them. Then, move forward! Reframe failure as a learning opportunity. With every failure, allow them to become a stepping stone that brings you closer to mastering your craft. Do not allow fear to paralyze you. Just stop doing that. Instead, use it as motivation to improve.

🖐️ Uncommon Mistake #2: Ignoring Your Well-being

In this industry, we constantly focus on our clients' happiness, but sometimes, we forget about ourselves. Self-care is important to your success. Just think, as travel professionals we offer and promote weekend getaways, wellness retreats, and other relaxation and rejuvenation experiences. Please, think of your emotional, mental, and physical self and your overall well-being. You can't serve your clients at your best if you're burned out.

Solution: Prioritize wellness and self-care. Make a realistic plan and schedule time for rest, exercise, and activities that recharge you. Remember, you're your most important asset. If you're not well, your business won't be either.

How does all this tie into your future success as a travel professional? These mistakes (both common and uncommon) are what will help you thrive when given thoughtful consideration and ultimately addressed. When you specialize, focus on relationships, and charge what you're worth, you'll attract the right clients looking for personalization and unique experiences. When you stop fearing failure and accept the of prioritizing your own well-being, you will have the endurance and resolve to push through challenges and obstacles. You will reach the end and celebrate the wins.

The good news is that success doesn't need to begin tomorrow. It starts today. Don't wait. Learn from mistakes and face, no, embrace these lessons and step into your future as a thriving successful travel professional.

From Sales Failure to Travel Success: A Journey of Growth and Resilience

When I started my travel business, I was excited yet overwhelmed. I envisioned helping people design memorable travel experiences, but reality quickly set in. Despite having a host agency providing me with leads, I struggled. My sales numbers were dismal, and I did not understand how to sell travel. Despite possessing a successful (award-winning) marketing and product development background in Corporate America and with non-profit organizations, I was a travel sales failure, plain and simple. But those early struggles shaped me, and in the end, they became the stepping stones to my success in selling group travel, women's wellness getaways, and luxury vacations.

⚠ Failure #1: The Fear of Rejection

Initially, I focused too much on the product and not enough on the people I was selling to, feeling that I could close the deal if I knew every detail about the destinations, hotels, and excursions. But no matter how much information I had, I couldn't convert the leads into actual bookings. Every time a potential client hesitated or showed resistance, I acquiesced or shut down. I didn't want to be a bother or thought that they did not want what I offered. I did not want to face or accept rejection and, as a result, didn't push through common objections and obstacles to close sales.

What I learned: Fear of failure taught me the importance of listening to clients and building trust, not just pitching a product. I realized rejection wasn't directed to me as a person, but to my lack of ability to clearly communicate in details to the client how I was delivering the travel experience they were looking for. It wasn't a personal attack, but a professional inadequate. It was part of the growth process. As a result, I stopped focusing solely on the sale and started focusing on the relationship. Instead of bombarding potential clients with facts, I began to understand their individualized concerns, needs, and wishes for an outstanding travel experience. I focused on how each client defined value and a successful trip. Once I started building genuine relationships, the sales started to increase.

⚠ Failure #2: The Mistake of Underpricing

Early on, I made another critical mistake. I undervalued myself and my services. I saw other travel agents competing for clients by offering lower prices, and I thought I had to do the same. I slashed my commissions and offered discounts to attract more customers. But the result? My clients didn't value my expertise or my time, and I found myself burnt out, working long hours for very little in return.

What I learned: This experience taught me that you get what you pay for in the travel industry, as in any business. Offering discounts and low prices undermined the value of the services I provided. As professionals, we offer expert travel advice, exceptional customer service along with personalized itineraries. Instead of competing on price, shift focus to value. We should always position ourselves as a professional travel advisor, offering experiences worth every penny. Charging what I was worth allowed me to work with clients who valued my expertise and were willing to pay for quality.

⚠ Failure #3: The Lack of a Niche

In my early days, I tried to be a "jack of all trades" and serve any client. I tried to take on all sorts of bookings—family vacations, honeymoons, and solo adventure travel- but I didn't specialize in anything. As a result, I couldn't stand out from the crowd. I spread myself too thin, became overwhelmed, and couldn't create the level of expertise or brand recognition that would help me succeed.

What I learned: Feeling the burn of not having a specialty was a turning point. I realized that to be truly successful, I needed to focus on a niche that excited my passion for travel: women's self-care and wellness. I began focusing on group travel and women's getaways and retreats, where I could leverage my strengths and offer truly bespoke services. I took the time to learn everything I could about these niches, built relationships with suppliers, and refined my approach to specific markets. By narrowing my focus, I attracted clients who valued my expertise and were willing to pay for tailored experiences.

The Turning Point: Turning Failures Into Success

Looking back on those failures, I see how essential they were to my growth. I became better at connecting with clients, more confident in charging my worth, and more focused on the niches that resonated with me. Today, my business sells group travel, women's getaways, and unforgettable vacations for clients. I've learned that failure isn't the end of the road, it's just the beginning of the next chapter.

My clients trust they get offered a unique, personalized experience, whether they're booking a rejuvenating wellness retreat or an extravagant getaway with friends. I'm no longer a "sales failure"; I am a travel advisor (travel expert) who knows how to deliver what my clients want and more.

What started as a string of failures became my greatest asset: the ability to empathize with clients, solve their travel problems, and curate experiences beyond their expectations. In the end, those early setbacks gave me the resilience and knowledge I needed to become the successful travel advisor and business owner I am today.

———————— • ————————

CHAPTER FOUR

*"In travel, every customer is an ambassador, and every journey is an
opportunity to create an extraordinary experience."*

–TANYA HOOT, FOUNDER OF THE HOOT GROUP

Fasten Your Seatbelt, Your Travel Business is About to Soar

As a travel professional and business owner, you bravely navigate the travel industry's far-reaching seas. With a passion for exploring new places, you envision success, knowing that your determination and willpower can sustain you. But here's the truth: while those qualities can drive you forward in the early stages of your journey, they are not enough to guarantee lasting success. The key to genuinely flying high in the travel business lies in understanding the deeper motivation behind why we got into this industry in the first place, yes, understanding our "why."

Just like a ship's captain needs to understand the correct path and prepare for the expedition ahead, we must always be clear about our purpose as travel professionals. The "why" is the foundation for all decisions, actions, and growth. Without it, a business might feel stuck in a holding pattern, making little progress despite your best efforts. With a clear sense of purpose, we must build a foundation to navigate any turbulence and rise above the challenges that come our way. Many travel business owners begin with passion and big dreams, whether offering personalized vacations, helping clients discover hidden gems, or simply sharing their love of travel. Dreams can fuel the journey, but the path will eventually require more than a dream. Our "why" will serve as the compass. It will also guide our decisions and help us prioritize essential actions.

Understanding our "why" means looking beyond the surface and identifying your business's core motivations. Is it financial freedom? A desire to help others or a yearning to make a positive impact in travel? Whatever it is, having a deeper understanding will allow you to break through the obstacles that could hold you back from more success. Aligning your business with your values. Stay true to your vision, and adapt to the changing landscape.

A travel business can soar higher than ever imagined, but only if you solidly understand why you're doing what you do. It's time to fasten your seatbelt because once you understand the "why," your journey is ready to take flight.

Habits for the Super Successful

Habits may seem like a simple idea, but they are critical for your travel business's growth and success. More specifically, it is vital to develop good habits that will set you apart and eliminate the bad habits that can hold you back.

As travel professionals, we understand the unique obstacles of this industry. Every day, we courageously confront the usual challenges: competition, ever-changing client needs, technology, and seasonal fluctuations. But there's one factor that remains constant: the power of habits. Good habits help you stay organized, increase efficiency, lead to increased sales, and, most importantly, build client trust. They are the backbone of long-term business success.

Habits, What Are They?

Let's start with a simple definition. According to the Merriam-Webster dictionary, a habit is "an acquired mode of behavior that has become nearly or completely involuntary." In other words, habits are actions you repeat regularly and often without thinking. The key here is that habits can either work for you or against you, so it's critical to cultivate good habits that will help you grow your travel business.

The Greek philosopher Aristotle reminds us of the power of habits:

"We are what we repeatedly do. Excellence, then, is not an act, but a habit."

This quote resonates deeply with travel professionals as business owners. One-time efforts don't achieve success in travel; it's cultivated over time through consistent, daily actions. But it's not just about working hard. It's about working smarter, and that's where your habits play a crucial role.

The Importance of Good Business Habits

As small business owners, you wear many hats: marketing, client relations, administration, budgeting, and more. The key to thriving in this environment is structure, and good habits help to create that structure. Successful business owners know that the foundation of long-term success is built upon consistent positive actions.

Let's take a moment to consider a few wise words from Maya Angelou, the late legendary writer and poet. She said, "We may encounter many defeats, but we must not be defeated."

Her quote reflects the importance of perseverance and consistency in business. It's easy to get discouraged, especially when working alone or facing a difficult market. But good habits empower us to push forward, learn from our mistakes, and ultimately create lasting success.

Five Habits Every
Travel Professionals Should Practice

Here are a few habits every travel professional and travel business owner should incorporate:

 ## Staying Organized:

Why? The travel industry is fast-paced. Successful use of calendars and CRM systems to keep track of bookings, customer preferences, deadlines, and much more requires accuracy and attention to detail.

 ## Prioritizing Client Relationships:

Why? Building strong relationships with clients is important to building a reputation. Having a business based on customer trust and the ability to provide personalized service will differentiate your travel services from the competition. A key habit is maintaining contact with clients. The action can be a simple follow-up, request for feedback, or recognizing personal milestones such as an anniversary or retirement.

 ## Continuous Learning:

Why? The travel industry changes rapidly. We can provide your clients with the best possible service and value by allowing ourselves time to learn about new destinations, offerings, technology, and travel trends. Continue to read industry blogs, attend webinars, and join professional associations and networks to stay ahead. We owe that to ourselves and the industry as professionals.

Effective Time Management:

Why? If operating a home-based business, it requires effective time management. Make it a habit to block out regular time for administrative duties, operational tasks, client calls, and marketing efforts. Scheduling will ensure you stay productive, accomplish daily tasks, and reduce the chance of becoming overwhelmed.

 ## Financial Discipline:

Why? Managing finances is the backbone of any business. Maintaining a budget, tracking expenses, and keeping your business finances separate from personal ones is essential. Healthy financial habits will enable your business to weather tough times and allow you to make informed decisions. Learn from the advice of reputable accounting and financial advisors.

Habits to Avoid in the Travel Business

While good habits can propel a business forward, bad habits can hinder progress. Here are a few habits to avoid:

 ## Procrastination:

Why? It's easy and takes little to no effort. Every business owner is guilty of it. However, putting off tasks may seem tempting when you're overwhelmed, but delaying critical activities, such as following up with leads or finalizing bookings, harms a business. Procrastination breeds unnecessary stress and missed opportunities.

👎 Ignoring Customer Feedback:

Why? Clients are the heart of the travel industry and your travel business. If you ignore their feedback, you miss the opportunity to improve. The old saying goes, "The customer is always right." The customer is not always right, but they are the customer. The goal is to make that one-time customer a long-term client. Whether it's a compliment or a complaint, take feedback seriously and make necessary adjustments to show your commitment to outstanding service.

👎 Neglecting Marketing:

Why? With any home-based business, regardless of industry, marketing is your lifeblood. Some owners believe that word-of-mouth will sustain them, but businesses can stagnate without an active marketing strategy (whether through social media, SEO, or local advertising). Marketing should be a regular habit, not something you do sporadically. Fortunately, you know that. That is why you are reading this book!

Focus on the habits that contribute to success in the travel industry and be mindful of the habits that could hold back growth. Habits can define a business. Make them count. Just as a traveler needs a map to reach their destination, habits are the compass that will guide business success in any industry, particularly the travel industry.

———— • ————

"My vision has always been to create a business where people feel empowered to explore the world with confidence."

—Kirsten A. M. Bär, Founder of Trafalgar

Harmony With the Travel Industry is Key to Survival and Success

The Importance of Travel Professionals Being in Harmony with the Travel Industry

In the competitive landscape of the travel industry, success is not just about offering enticing deals or special promotions but also about understanding the dynamics of the industry itself and aligning with it. As travel professionals become more aligned with the travel industry, they will have a broad understanding and the ability to navigate trends, adapt to changing demands, and take advantage of wide-ranging best practices.

What Does it Mean to Be in Harmony with the Travel Industry?

As briefly mentioned previously, harmony in any industry requires alignment. In the travel industry, harmony often refers to aligning operations, values, and strategies with broader trends, innovations, and demands. A travel professional in harmony with the industry can effectively navigate challenges with consumer behaviors, economic downturns, technological shifts, and evolving consumer behaviors. Harmony requires maintaining strong relationships with travel suppliers, quickly adapting to customer preferences and expectations, and staying informed about industry shifts. It also requires adopting industry best practices.

Ways Industry Harmony Is Established:

Adapting to Consumer Trends: Understanding and meeting the evolving preferences of travelers, from sustainable travel to digital-first experiences.

Using Industry Tools and Innovations: Leveraging technological advancements such as booking platforms, customer relationship management (CRM) systems, and data analytics to improve service delivery and customer engagement.

Maintaining Strong Supplier Relationships: Collaborating with airlines, hotels, and local operators to offer exclusive deals and packages.

Compliance with Industry Regulations: Ensuring the business meets legal and ethical standards, such as safety protocols and environmental regulations.

Why Is Being in Harmony with the Travel Industry Essential?

Harmony with the travel industry is essential for several reasons. These include staying competitive, fostering customer loyalty, improving operational efficiency, and ensuring sustainable growth.

👍 Competitiveness in the Market

In a highly competitive industry like travel, staying in harmony with the industry's trends and innovations is crucial for maintaining competitiveness. Businesses that are out of touch with industry developments may fall behind their competitors, failing to capitalize on new opportunities. For example, many travel businesses today are shifting to digital platforms to serve tech-savvy customers. A travel business that ignores this trend risks losing market share to more tech-forward competitors.

The rise of online travel agencies (OTAs) such as Expedia, Booking.com, and Airbnb has fundamentally reshaped the travel landscape. These companies have adapted quickly to technological advancements, customer preferences, and emerging trends. They have streamlined the booking process and offered customers a seamless online experience, positioning themselves as leaders in the industry. A travel business in harmony with such shifts can leverage the same technologies, offer similar customer experiences, and remain competitive.

👍 Meeting Customer Expectations

Traveler expectations have shifted dramatically in recent years, driven by the rise of low-cost airlines, increasing interest in sustainable travel, and the growing importance of digital experiences. To remain relevant in the travel industry, travel professionals must understand these expectations and adapt their offerings accordingly.

For example, the growing demand for sustainable tourism has led many travelers to seek environmentally responsible options. A travel business that does not align with this trend may lose customers who prioritize sustainability. On the other hand, a company that aligns with the trend could attract new customers by offering eco-friendly travel packages, such as trips that emphasize local culture, support for green hotels, or carbon offsetting options.

Moreover, customer service expectations in the travel industry have increased. Travelers today expect personalized, 24/7 customer service and instant booking options. Travel business owners who understand and embrace these demands will likely retain loyal customers and secure repeat business.

👍 Operational Efficiency

When travel professionals align with industry trends, they can also improve the efficiency of their operations. Alignment includes automating booking systems, using data to understand customer preferences better, and streamlining internal processes to reduce costs. Businesses that fail to adopt such technologies and practices may find themselves less efficient, incurring higher operational costs and ultimately lowering profitability.

For instance, many travel businesses use advanced CRM tools to manage customer relationships better and gain insights into customer behavior. These tools help businesses personalize marketing efforts and improve customer retention. Companies that neglect such technological advancements risk falling behind in an increasingly data-driven industry.

👍 Growth and Profitability

Maintaining harmony with the travel industry also contributes to long-term growth and profitability. Travel businesses that identify and capitalize on emerging trends early have the potential to lead the market and create new revenue streams. For example, the rise of niche tourism markets, such as adventure tourism, wellness travel, and culinary tourism, offers businesses an opportunity to diversify their product offerings and attract a wider audience.

Conversely, businesses that resist change or ignore industry trends often struggle with stagnation or decline. This stagnation can be particularly true in the travel industry, where shifts in consumer preferences and technological advancements can rapidly alter the market.

An Example of a Travel Business in Harmony with the Industry

A prime example of a travel business that is ideally in harmony with industry is Airbnb. Founded in 2008, Airbnb has successfully navigated the changing landscape of the travel industry by recognizing early the growing desire for unique, personalized travel experiences. Unlike traditional hotels, Airbnb capitalized on the increasing demand for more authentic, local, and cost-effective accommodations. Over time, the company expanded its offerings to include "Airbnb Experiences," allowing travelers to book local tours, activities, and events. This expansion was in perfect harmony with the rise of experiential travel (where tourists seek deeper cultural connections).

Airbnb also embraced technology to enhance customer experience, offering a seamless booking, payment, and communication platform between hosts and guests. It has continuously adapted to consumer preferences, incorporating flexible booking options, instant booking, and guest reviews to build trust within the community (Hempel, J. (2016). How Airbnb conquered the world—and turned its CEO into a billion-dollar mogul. Fortune Magazine. *https://fortune.com/2016/06/02/airbnb-ceo-brian-chesky-interview/*).

The company also addressed evolving regulatory challenges, working with local governments and lawmakers to ensure compliance while maintaining the essence of its platform. By staying connected to industry shifts and responding to consumer demands, Airbnb continues to grow and expand globally, remaining a dominant player in the travel sector.

Example of a Travel Business
Out of Harmony with the Industry

Thomas Cook is an example of a travel business that some business analysts believed struggled due to being out of harmony with the travel industry. Founded in 1841, Thomas Cook was once one of the most iconic names in travel, providing package holidays to millions of customers worldwide. However, the company failed to adapt to significant shifts in the travel industry, particularly the rise of online booking platforms and the changing preferences of younger, tech-savvy travelers.

One of Thomas Cook's key missteps was its failure to embrace the growing trend of online travel booking and the increasing demand for personalized, flexible travel options. While online travel agencies such as Expedia and Booking.com adapted quickly to digital transformation, Thomas Cook continued to rely heavily on physical stores and traditional booking methods. The slow realignment made it increasingly difficult for the company to compete with more agile, tech-focused competitors.

Additionally, the company was slow to respond to changing customer preferences, particularly the demand for sustainable travel options and more customized experiences. As a result, Thomas Cook struggled to attract younger generations of travelers who were more likely to book their trips online and prioritize sustainability.

In 2019, Thomas Cook went into liquidation, marking the end of a once-powerful brand that failed to evolve (Brown, R. (2019). Thomas Cook: The collapse of a global travel giant. BBC News. *https://www.bbc.com/news/uk-49804261)*. This collapse is a cautionary tale about the risks of being out of harmony with the travel industry.

A travel business owner's ability to stay in harmony with the travel industry is essential to long-term success, increased sales, and sustained profitability. By staying aware of industry trends, leveraging technological advancements, meeting consumer demands, and maintaining strong supplier relationships, business owners can navigate the complexities of the travel sector and stay competitive. Conversely, those who fail to adapt to industry shifts risk falling behind, as demonstrated by the collapse of Thomas Cook. Businesses like Airbnb, which have embraced change and aligned themselves with evolving trends, continue to thrive in a rapidly changing marketplace. Therefore, the importance of harmony between a travel business and the industry cannot be overstated, and it is crucial for growth, relevance, and lasting success.

Travel Industry Consumer Trends into 2040: What to Expect to Ensure Business Survival and Profit

As the travel industry evolves, business owners must stay informed and adaptable to emerging consumer trends to ensure their survival and profitability. Between 2025 and 2040, several key shifts are expected to reshape the travel landscape. By understanding and aligning with these trends, travel businesses can position themselves for success in an increasingly competitive and dynamic market. This chapter will explore three significant consumer trends expected to shape the future of travel and explain how businesses can remain in harmony with these trends for long-term growth and profitability.

 ## Sustainability and Eco-Friendly Travel

Sustainability is rapidly becoming a top priority for consumers, and this trend will accelerate during the next 15 to 20 years, now and into 2040. Travelers, especially younger generations such as Millennials and Gen Z, increasingly prioritize eco-friendly transportation, accommodation, and activity options. According to a 2023 report by Booking.com, nearly 74% of global travelers intend to make more sustainable travel choices, indicating a clear shift toward environmentally responsible tourism (Booking.com, 2023). This trend will likely intensify in the coming years as consumers become more aware of the environmental impacts of their travel choices.

For travel professionals, understanding the importance of sustainability is crucial to staying in harmony with the industry. Businesses can remain competitive by offering eco-conscious travel packages, such as carbon-neutral flights, stays at sustainable hotels, and tours focused on environmental preservation. Additionally, promoting responsible tourism practices, such as supporting local communities and wildlife conservation efforts, will appeal to the growing demand for sustainable travel experiences. Incorporating sustainability into the core of a business model not only helps attract eco-minded consumers but also fosters long-term loyalty as travelers increasingly seek brands that align with their values.

For example, Intrepid Travel, a tour operator specializing in adventure travel, has made sustainability a central focus. The company has committed to reducing its carbon footprint by offsetting emissions, supporting local businesses, and promoting responsible tourism practices (Intrepid Travel, 2023). This commitment has resonated with environmentally conscious travelers, contributing to the company's success.

 # Technology and Personalization

As technology continues to advance, consumers are increasingly expecting personalized travel experiences. By 2025, the integration of artificial intelligence (AI), data analytics, and virtual reality (VR) will likely be essential in shaping the future of travel. Travelers will demand seamless, customized experiences, with AI-driven recommendations, personalized itineraries, and digital concierge services becoming the norm. A 2022 report from McKinsey & Company found that 70% of travelers prefer personalized recommendations, and 60% expect a personalized experience throughout their trip (McKinsey & Company, 2022).

To remain in harmony with the industry, travel businesses must embrace technology to enhance the customer experience. This is achieved by leveraging AI to offer tailored suggestions based on past travel behavior, preferences, and budget. Integrating technology like chatbots for instant customer service, virtual tours to preview destinations, and intelligent booking systems can improve convenience and satisfaction. Businesses that provide easy-to-use apps and websites that offer real-time travel updates and utilize data to predict consumer needs will stand out in an increasingly tech-driven market.

Expedia Group offers a prime example of a travel business using technology to personalize experiences. The company utilizes AI to tailor travelers' recommendations based on previous bookings and browsing behavior. At the same time, its mobile app allows users to manage bookings, access personalized travel deals, and receive real-time notifications about their trips (Expedia Group, 2023). By integrating advanced technologies, Expedia remains a leader in the travel industry, providing customers with a seamless, personalized experience.

Experience-Driven Travel

The shift from traditional sightseeing to experience-driven travel is another significant trend expected to define the travel industry from 2025 to 2040. Consumers increasingly seek authentic, immersive experiences rather than just visiting popular landmarks. A study by the U.S. Travel Association found that 58% of travelers consider cultural and authentic experiences as the most important aspect of their travel (U.S. Travel Association, 2022). This trend reflects the growing desire among travelers to connect with local cultures, engage in adventure tourism, and seek unique, off-the-beaten-path activities.

For travel businesses, it is essential to understand this shift and cater to the demand for unique, experiential travel options. This can involve offering local and cultural tours, culinary experiences, wellness retreats, or adventure travel packages. By providing personalized experiences beyond typical tourist attractions, businesses can appeal to travelers looking for meaningful and memorable trips. This also includes creating opportunities for travelers to engage with local communities in a way that promotes responsible tourism and fosters cultural exchange.

A company like Airbnb has already capitalized on this trend by expanding its offerings to include "Airbnb Experiences," which allow travelers to participate in unique local activities such as cooking classes, guided hikes, and art workshops. By prioritizing authentic, experience-based travel, Airbnb has differentiated itself from traditional accommodation providers and tapped into the growing demand for immersive travel experiences (Airbnb, 2023).

In short, the travel industry will undergo significant transformations between 2025 and 2040, driven by evolving consumer expectations. To stay in harmony with these changes, travel businesses must adapt to key trends such as sustainability, technology-driven personalization, and the increasing demand for authentic, experience-driven travel. By aligning with these trends, businesses can not only meet the evolving needs of consumers but also position themselves for long-term success and profitability.

Sustainability will be at the forefront of consumer decision-making, and businesses that embrace eco-friendly practices will have a competitive edge. Personalization through technology will become essential, with businesses using AI and data analytics to deliver tailored experiences. Finally, the demand for unique, immersive travel experiences will drive the industry toward more personalized and authentic offerings. By staying attuned to these trends and adapting their strategies accordingly, travel businesses can ensure their survival and profitability in an ever-changing market.

---•---

CHAPTER SIX

"Opportunities don't happen. You create them."

— CHRIS GROSSER, AUTHOR, ENTREPRENEUR, MOTIVATIONAL SPEAKER

How to Network When You Hate Networking

The Importance of Business Networking for Business Owners Who Are Intimidated by It

Networking is a critical skill for business owners, especially in industries like travel, where relationships and partnerships can significantly impact growth, client acquisition, and long-term success. However, many business professionals find networking intimidating or uncomfortable, particularly those who are introverted or do not enjoy small talk. Truth is, I was like that! Despite these feelings, networking is not about making new friends (but you do) or having surface-level conversations. It is about building meaningful, strategic relationships that can directly contribute to business success. For travel professionals, networking is essential for growth, collaboration, and profitability. So, go ahead, do it!

This chapter explores the importance of networking, especially for professionals who find it challenging, with a specific focus on the travel industry. Then, easy-to-follow steps are suggested to make networking more approachable and successful. Lastly, an example of how a travel professional can use networking to grow their email marketing list. Email marketing is one tool that is often considered crucial for client engagement and long-term profitability.

Understanding the Importance of Networking

Networking offers many benefits for business owners. When done effectively, it helps travel professionals build a network, provide opportunities to learn from others, exchange valuable information, and even create potential collaborations. Let's dive deeper into why networking is worthwhile and doesn't have to be intimidating.

1. Client Acquisition and Retention

One of the most significant benefits of networking is client acquisition or more customers! Travel professionals who network regularly have access to a larger pool of potential clients. Networking allows a professional to meet people who could benefit from their products and services, turning these connections into leads.

For travel businesses, the stakes are even higher. Customers and long-term clients look for personalized, trusted recommendations and services. Developing a reliable network of peers, potential collaborators, and reputable travel industry contacts can provide introductions and referrals. Strong networking connections can also help retain clients through consistent engagement, support, and additional offers.

2. Collaborations and Partnerships

Networking opens the door to mutually beneficial collaborations and partnerships. In the travel industry, collaboration is key, whether it's partnering with other travel agents, hotels, tour operators, or destination marketing organizations (DMOs). Collaborations can enhance services, increase business visibility, and ultimately drive growth.

Here's an example. A travel professional can collaborate with a hotel to offer exclusive deals to their clients. Likewise, working with local businesses in popular vacation destinations can create cross-promotions, where each partner benefits from increased exposure and shared resources.

3. Vendor Relations and Supply Chain Management

Strong vendor relationships are a cornerstone of success for travel professionals. Travel advisors, tour operators, and agencies often rely on third-party vendors, such as airlines, hotels, transportation services, and activity providers, to deliver comprehensive travel packages to clients. By building solid relationships with these vendors, business owners can negotiate better deals, secure discounts, and ensure their clients a more seamless travel experience.

Networking with vendors can help a travel professional establish credibility, gain early access to new offers, and ensure reliable delivery of services, which is crucial for long-term success.

4. Industry Knowledge and Insights

Continue to learn from others! Networking isn't just about gaining business; it is also about learning. The travel industry is ever evolving, with trends, consumer preferences, and regulations constantly shifting. By networking with others in the industry, travel professionals can stay updated on emerging trends, best practices, and new technologies that may enhance their business operations or marketing strategies.

Attending travel industry conferences, participating in webinars, and engaging with other professionals in travel-related online forums can provide constant opportunities to learn and gain the knowledge and insights necessary to stay competitive in a fast-paced industry.

5. Increased Profits and Opportunities

Networking can directly influence profits. When done strategically, business owners can leverage their relationships to generate new revenue streams. For example, imagine a travel advisor connecting with a destination marketing organization to secure exclusive packages or collaborating with a popular travel blogger to promote their services.

By diversifying income sources through partnerships and leveraging the network for promotions, referrals, and direct sales, travel professionals are poised to experience growth in both revenue and profit.

Overcoming the Intimidation of Networking

While the benefits of networking are clear, many travel professionals and business owners remain intimidated by the idea. The thought of attending events, introducing oneself to strangers, or initiating conversations can cause discomfort.

Do any of the following reasons resonate? Here are a few reasons why travel professionals might fear networking and solutions to overcome these barriers:

Fear of Rejection

One of the primary reasons people are intimidated by networking is the fear of rejection. The idea that others might not be interested in building a relationship or that they could face a negative response makes some people hesitant to reach out. That is normal.

Solution: Reframe networking as an opportunity to offer value rather than focusing solely on what you can get from it. Approach every conversation as a potential opportunity to learn, offer assistance, or share insights. Remember that rejection isn't personal; it is professional and part of the process. Have you ever rejected an idea, partnership, or collaboration that wasn't right for you or your business? You most likely did not dislike the person; it just wasn't the right fit. It isn't personal!

Lack of Confidence

For many, the idea of "selling" themselves as travel professionals or the packages they offer can be daunting. Without confidence in their product offerings and services, travel professionals may shy away from promoting their business.

Solution: Focus on your expertise and the value you bring to the travel. Who you are and what you offer is valuable and adds to the travel industry. Start with small, low-pressure interactions and gradually build confidence over time. Preparation is key, so practice your elevator pitch, anticipate common questions, and be ready to talk about what makes your business unique.

Perceived Time Commitment

Networking is perceived as an overwhelming time investment. Many business owners, including travel professionals, feel that networking takes them away from the operational side of their business, which could be a significant deterrent.

Solution: View networking as an investment, not a chore. Even small networking efforts, such as having one productive weekly conversation, can yield great returns. Additionally, many networking opportunities can be integrated into your existing schedule, for example, connecting with industry professionals at travel-related conferences or meetings you attend.

Overwhelming Social Situations

Some people find social situations like conferences, after-hour socials, or industry events overwhelming, especially if the settings are large and unstructured.

Solution: Start with smaller events or one-on-one meetings, which can feel more manageable. Set goals for each event, whether connecting with one new person or learning about a new opportunity. Over time, these smaller, focused interactions can build your network without feeling overwhelming.

Easy Steps to Successful Networking in the Travel Industry

Now that we've established why networking is essential and how to overcome common barriers, let's look at practical steps that travel professionals can take to become successful at networking, particularly within the travel industry.

☑ Step 1: Leverage Existing Relationships

Start by focusing on the connections you already have. You might have friends, family, or past clients connected to potential collaborators, vendors, or clients in the travel industry. Reach out to these individuals and ask for introductions. Networking doesn't always have to start from scratch. It can often be about tapping into the network that already exists.

For example, if you're a travel advisor, ask clients who have had positive experiences to refer you to their friends or family. You could offer them a discount or incentive for each successful referral, encouraging further networking through word of mouth.

☑ Step 2: Attend Industry Events and Conferences

Conferences and trade shows provide an excellent opportunity for in-person networking with vendors, potential partners, and clients. Even if you're not an extrovert, attending travel industry events can help you meet the right people in a more structured setting. Be prepared to introduce yourself quickly and clearly, always with a business card or digital contact tool ready to share.

For travel professionals, attending events hosted by organizations such as the American Society of Travel Advisors (ASTA), Cruise Lines International Association (CLIA), The Travel Institute, International Airlines Travel Agent Network (IATAN), or the Travel Leaders Network and other travel industry recognized organizations can help build meaningful industry relationships.

☑ Step 3: Utilize Social Media and Online Communities

If in-person networking feels intimidating, social media platforms like LinkedIn, Facebook, and Instagram provide great opportunities to network without leaving the comfort of your office. Join travel industry-related groups, engage with posts, share valuable content, and participate in discussions. Establish yourself as a knowledgeable resource and build a digital network that translates into real-world business opportunities.

Travel professionals can join online communities for travel advisors and niche travel interests, such as those on Facebook, where they can share tips, collaborate on business opportunities, and discuss new industry trends.

☑ Step 4: Follow Up and Stay Engaged

Networking is not just about making initial contact; it's how relationships are established to grow over time. After meeting someone, always follow up with a personalized message expressing gratitude for the conversation. Also, suggest ways you could work together in the future. It is important to stay engaged with your network, whether through email or social media. These touchpoints ensure you remain "top of mind" when new opportunities arise.

☑ Step 5: Focus on Building Authentic Relationships, Not Just Sales

A professional does not need to close a sale during every conversation or interaction. Do not fall into that faulty thinking. It is more advantageous to focus on building genuine relationships. What can you bring to the relationship? Offer value, ask questions, and learn from others. Over time, these authentic connections will create new opportunities for collaboration, referrals, and growth.

Growing Your Email Marketing List through Networking

Email marketing is one of the most effective ways to engage with clients, and networking can play a critical role in growing an email list. For a travel advisor, this could involve networking at industry events or through digital platforms and asking for permission to send helpful content, special offers, or travel tips.

Here's an example of how a travel advisor can network to grow their email marketing list:

Attend a local travel expo or industry event: Interact with potential clients or partners, offering exclusive and valuable advice or deals in exchange for email sign-ups.

Offer a free resource or travel guide: Create valuable content, such as a free destination guide or travel checklist, and offer it to individuals in exchange for their email addresses.

Referral Program: Encourage current clients to refer friends in exchange for special offers or discounts. Ask clients to provide email addresses for referrals, expanding the reach of the advisor's email list.

Email Follow-up: After the event or meeting, send a personalized email thanking the individual for their time and offering them additional content or a special offer in exchange for their subscription to your newsletter.

A travel advisor should leverage networking opportunities to build an engaged and interested email marketing list. Do not let the opportunity to boost client retention and increase future sales and revenue pass you by.

Networking may seem intimidating to business owners who are not naturally inclined toward relationship-building, but it is a vital skill that can help grow any business, especially in industries like travel. Overcome your hesitation. By embracing networking to build meaningful relationships, business owners can enhance client acquisition, create valuable partnerships, and ultimately drive higher profits. Follow the steps outlined in this chapter to become a travel professional who develops a successful network. These efforts can lead to long-term success, including growing a robust email marketing list to drive future engagement and sales.

———————— • ————————

CHAPTER SEVEN

*"Marketing is no longer about the
stuff you make, but the stories you tell."*

—SETH GODIN, AUTHOR AND MARKETING EXPERT

Level the Playing Field
with Marketing

The Importance of Marketing
to Travel Professionals

Marketing is a cornerstone of business success, acting as the bridge between products and potential customers. This is especially true for the travel industry, where competition is often fierce, and customer loyalty is paramount. The travel industry has undergone substantial changes in the past few decades, including agencies and tour operators to hotel chains, cruise lines, and online platforms. The global market is more connected than ever. Yet, the challenges for small and large travel businesses remain remarkably similar: how to reach the right customer, create lasting relationships, and stand out in a crowded market.

This chapter delves into the importance of marketing for travel business owners, explains the evolution of marketing in the past 20 years, and provides a comprehensive, easy-to-follow marketing strategy for a new travel business. Additionally, this chapter includes an example of a travel advisor who successfully grew her business despite a significant challenge in her multi-generational cruise niche. Finally, we will outline five key marketing "musts" that every travel business should adopt to level the playing field.

 # What is Marketing and Marketing Management?

Before diving into marketing specifics for travel professionals, it's worthwhile to understand the proper discipline of marketing and marketing management.

Marketing: Definition and Scope

At its core, marketing involves the activities and processes for creating, communicating, delivering, and exchanging offerings that have value for customers, clients, partners, and society. It is a strategic process that identifies and understands the needs and wants of target customers. Then, marketers create products or services that satisfy these needs, communicate their value to the customer, and deliver them in a way that creates a positive customer experience.

Within the travel industry, marketing could include advertising a new vacation package, promoting discounted hotel rooms, creating social media campaigns to raise awareness about a destination, or offering a limited-time deal on an all-inclusive resort. Travel professionals also use marketing to engage existing customers, encourage repeat bookings, and build customer loyalty.

Travel Marketing Management

Marketing management in travel is crucial because it involves making decisions about the positioning of travel products, the strategies used to attract new customers, and how customer relationships are built and maintained. This requires understanding the travel product offerings and the target customer's behavior. It involves setting marketing goals, determining the marketing mix (product, price, place, promotion), analyzing market trends and competition, and continuously adapting the strategy to changing conditions.

The Evolution of Marketing in the Past 20 Years and How it Affects the Travel Industry

The marketing field has evolved significantly in the past 20 years, and the travel industry has not been immune to these changes. The rise of digital technologies, the growth of online platforms, and the shift in consumer behavior have transformed how travel businesses market themselves.

The Rise of Digital Marketing

In the early 2000s, marketing was largely traditional: print ads, TV commercials, and direct mail. However, digital marketing began to take center stage with the advent of the Internet and the rise of social media platforms. Travel businesses no longer had to rely on expensive television commercials or print brochures; instead, they could use targeted online ads, search engine optimization (SEO), email marketing, and social media to reach their audience.

One of the most significant shifts in the past 20 years has been how consumers research and book travel. In the past, travel agencies were the gatekeepers of travel knowledge, offering personalized recommendations and itineraries. Today, consumers have access to a wealth of information at their fingertips, from review websites like TripAdvisor to booking engines like Expedia and Airbnb. As a result, travel businesses have had to adapt, providing more personalized digital experiences while also finding ways to capture the attention of potential customers online.

Social Media and User-Generated Content

Social media platforms like Facebook, Instagram, Twitter, and YouTube have reshaped how travel businesses interact with customers. Social media is now a primary channel for communication and marketing, where companies can engage with customers in real-time. User-generated content, such as reviews, photos, and videos posted by satisfied customers, has also become a key element of modern travel marketing.

Travel businesses must leverage social media and create campaigns encouraging customers to share their travel experiences. Additionally, many travel companies use influencer marketing, partnering with travel bloggers and social media influencers to promote destinations, products, or services to a broader audience.

The Advent of Data Analytics and Personalization

Data analytics has become an integral part of modern marketing. Travel businesses can now track and analyze customer behavior, preferences, and booking patterns to create highly targeted campaigns. By understanding which customers are most likely to book certain types of travel, businesses can tailor their marketing efforts to appeal to specific market segments.

Personalization has become a key trend in the travel industry, with customers expecting individualized experiences. For example, a travel advisor may use customer data to offer personalized travel recommendations based on previous trips, interests, or special events such as birthdays or anniversaries. Marketing automation tools have made it easier for travel businesses to send personalized emails, create dynamic website content, and develop custom offers tailored to customers' needs.

Mobile Marketing and the Shift to Mobile Booking

The shift to mobile has been one of the most significant changes in the past two decades. Smartphones have revolutionized how consumers book and plan their travel, making it essential for travel businesses to optimize their websites and marketing efforts for mobile devices. Many travelers now book their flights, hotels, and activities directly from their smartphones, often using apps or booking platforms such as Airbnb or Skyscanner.

This shift to mobile has also impacted how businesses reach their customers. SMS marketing, mobile app notifications, and location-based promotions are commonplace in the travel industry. Businesses that fail to optimize for mobile devices risk losing a large portion of their target audience.

Influence of Sustainability and Ethical Marketing

Over the past two decades, consumers have become increasingly aware of environmental and social issues, leading to a rise in demand for sustainable and ethical travel options. Travel businesses now promote eco-friendly practices, sustainable tourism, and responsible travel experiences. This has led to a new type of marketing known as "ethical marketing," where businesses emphasize their commitment to sustainability and social responsibility.

Sustainability has become a selling point for many travel brands, and customers now expect businesses to be transparent about their practices and contribute positively to their communities.

A Complete Marketing Strategy for a New Travel Business

Starting a new travel business requires a well-thought-out marketing strategy to ensure success. Below is a step-by-step approach to creating an effective marketing strategy.

☑ Step 1: Define Your Target Audience

Before you start any marketing efforts, it's essential to identify your target customers. Are you targeting adventure travelers, luxury vacationers, or family holidaymakers? Defining your target audience will help you tailor your marketing messages, choose the right channels, and create content that resonates with your potential customers.

☑ Step 2: Develop a Strong Brand Identity

Your brand is how customers perceive your business, and creating a strong, unique brand identity is crucial. Your brand should reflect your travel business's values, mission, and personality. This includes developing a logo, choosing brand colors, crafting a compelling tagline, and designing a user-friendly website. Consistency in branding across all marketing channels is key to building trust and recognition with your audience.

☑ Step 3: Build an Online Presence

In today's digital age, having a strong online presence is non-negotiable. This involves having a professional website optimized for SEO and mobile devices. Your website should include information about your services, destination guides, customer testimonials, and an easy-to-navigate booking system.

In addition to your website, you should have a presence on social media platforms like Instagram, Facebook, and Twitter. Regularly post engaging content, such as destination highlights, travel tips, customer testimonials, and special promotions. Social media provides a unique opportunity to connect with potential customers and build a community around your brand.

☑ Step 4: Utilize Email Marketing

Email marketing remains one of the most effective ways to engage with potential and existing customers. Start by building an email list through lead generation tactics such as offering a free travel guide, discounts, or exclusive offers in exchange for email sign-ups. Use email marketing to send personalized travel recommendations, promotions, and content that provides value to your audience.

☑ Step 5: Implement Paid Advertising

While organic marketing efforts are essential, paid advertising can help accelerate the growth of your new travel business. Consider running paid ads on social media platforms like Facebook and Instagram and using Google Ads to target potential customers who are actively searching for travel services.

☑ Step 6: Monitor and Adjust

Marketing is an ongoing process, and it's crucial to track the performance of your efforts. Use analytics tools to monitor website traffic, social media engagement, email open rates, and the ROI of paid ads. Based on this data, adjust your strategy to improve your results over time.

Example: a Multi-Generational Cruise Travel Advisor

Consider the example of a travel advisor specializing in multi-generational cruise travel. This niche market targets families who want to plan vacations with multiple generations, from grandparents to grandchildren. The advisor faced the common challenge of standing out in a highly competitive cruise industry and appealing to families with diverse needs and preferences.

To overcome this challenge, the advisor focused on creating personalized travel packages that catered to the specific needs of each family member, from child-friendly activities to luxury dining experiences for adults. She used email marketing to build relationships with potential customers, offering expert advice on family-friendly cruise options and creating content that resonated with her audience.

By leveraging social media platforms like Instagram and Facebook, she shared family vacation success stories, user-generated content, and promotions. She also collaborated with cruise lines to offer exclusive deals, further strengthening her relationships within the industry.

Through these efforts, she successfully grew her client base and differentiated herself from other travel advisors in the cruise market.

Five Must-Have Tactics for Marketing a Travel Business

Optimize Your Online Presence: In today's digital world, your website and social media presence are essential. Make sure your website is professional, mobile-friendly, and optimized for SEO. Regularly post engaging content on social media to build brand awareness and customer loyalty.

Leverage Email Marketing: Build an email list to send personalized recommendations, promotions, and travel tips. Email marketing is one of the most effective ways to convert leads into paying customers and build long-term relationships.

Invest in Paid Advertising: Use paid social media and Google advertising to reach a broader audience. Paid ads can drive traffic to your website and help generate more leads for your travel business.

Offer Value Through Content: Create valuable content that educates, entertains, or inspires your target audience. Whether through blogs, videos, or social media posts, content marketing helps position your business as a trusted authority in the travel industry.

Build Strategic Partnerships: Collaborate with other businesses, such as hotels, airlines, and tour operators, to offer bundled services or exclusive deals. Partnerships can help you expand your reach and provide additional value to your customers.

By implementing these actions, your travel businesses can build lasting customer relationships, ultimately leveling the playing field in a constantly evolving industry.

CHAPTER EIGHT

*"Your brand is what other people say about
you when you're not in the room."*

—JEFF BEZOS, FOUNDER OF AMAZON

More Momentum. A Marketing Makeover for Your Travel Business

Build Marketing Momentum

In the big world of travel, the vista continues to evolve. As a travel professional with an agency or in the role of a travel advisor, it can be easy to feel that current marketing efforts are sufficient. It could be the opposite; the marketing strategies and tactics are insufficient. It's necessary to regularly review your efforts and strategies to refine and adjust those in place. The travel industry is dynamic, and the way travelers make decisions, book trips, and seek advice from travel experts has transformed during the past few years. Whether it's the rise of social media, the growing reliance on online reviews, or the introduction of new technology, businesses, including travel businesses, must adapt to stay relevant.

This chapter explores how travel professionals can undertake a "marketing makeover" to increase the momentum and profitability of their businesses. Do not think of abandoning the strategies that have succeeded thus far. Instead, refine existing marketing practices. As a travel professional, the key to success is recognizing that minor adjustments can significantly impact long-term growth. Take the time to focus on specific areas for improvement. As a travel professional, set yourself apart in a crowded industry by engaging target audiences more effectively. It will boost sales.

Seven Recommendations for Giving Your Travel Business a Marketing Makeover That will Create Momentum and Drive Profits:

1. Refine Your Brand Identity and Brand Messaging

Marketing campaigns begin with understanding your identity: who you are, what you offer, and how you offer it. Does your identity speak to your ideal customers? Identity is your brand. And your brand is you. How would your clients or potential customers describe you and your business? What adjectives would they use? When contemplating purchasing, travelers rely heavily on trust and personalized recommendations. A brand goes beyond a logo or a name; it represents who you are and what you offer.

Recommendation: Review and refine your brand's message, aesthetics, and tone. Ask yourself, "Does my current brand communicate the value I offer?" Ensure the brand is engaging and distinct enough to stand out in a crowded market.

Example: If you run a niche travel agency specializing in eco-friendly vacations, your brand must communicate this message across all platforms, from social media posts to the website. Use a green color palette, eco-conscious language, and visuals that reflect your sustainable travel experiences. Your brand messaging could include statements like "Sustainable vacations that protect the planet," highlighting how your services align with travelers' values.

Benefit: A refined and cohesive brand identity helps you establish a more apparent position in the market, making it easier to attract your ideal clients. It fosters trust with potential clients and sets the stage for more loyal, repeat business.

2. Appreciate the Impact of Social Media Marketing

Social media is a powerful tool for increasing visibility, building client relationships, and driving sales. For travel advisors, it offers the perfect platform to showcase destinations, share travel tips, and connect with potential customers personally. Social media platforms can be fundamental for building brand awareness. With billions of digital users worldwide, social media provides a huge opportunity for developing customer relationships and boosting growth.

Recommendation: Shift from simply posting promotional content to providing valuable and engaging information. Create a social media calendar that includes travel tips, destination highlights, behind-the-scenes content, client testimonials, and user-generated content. Incorporate storytelling to make your posts resonate with your audience.

Example: If you specialize in luxury cruises, share customer testimonials showcasing their unique and amazing experiences. Post stunning photos of cruise destinations, insider tips on booking luxury cruises, and updates on new offers or itineraries. Have you engaged with your followers by asking questions like, "What's your dream cruise destination?" and sharing polls or quizzes to encourage interaction.

Benefit: Engaging with potential clients on social media builds relationships and positions you as a travel expert. You can increase brand awareness and client loyalty by showcasing your knowledge and expertise, leading to higher conversion rates.

3. Implement Content Marketing and SEO Strategies

Content marketing is one of the most effective ways to build trust with your audience while improving your visibility on search engines. SEO (Search Engine Optimization) strategies help ensure potential clients find you when searching for travel-related information. Content marketing remains an invaluable tool for travel businesses. A blog or video series can position you as an expert in your niche while providing helpful information to potential clients. Create high-quality, relevant content to provide value, improve your SEO, and engage your audience.

Recommendation: Develop a content marketing strategy that revolves around writing high-quality blogs, creating videos, and optimizing your website for SEO. Do your current marketing efforts focus on answering common questions and solving problems for your target audience? By strategically placing keywords and providing valuable content, you will most likely increase your chances of ranking higher on search engines.

Example: If you specialize in family vacations, write blog posts like "10 Best Family-Friendly Destinations for Summer 2024" or "How to Plan a Stress-Free Family Vacation." Use SEO tools to find keywords related to family vacations and include them in your blog posts and website.

Benefit: SEO and content marketing drive organic traffic to your website, improving visibility without needing paid ads. Well-crafted content also nurtures your relationship with clients, positioning your business as an expert in the travel industry.

4. Refocus Your Email Marketing Campaigns

Email marketing remains one of the most effective tools for customer retention and nurturing leads. Travel advisors often focus on generating new clients, but it's equally important to maintain relationships with existing clients and past travelers.

Recommendation: Create targeted email campaigns that are personalized and segmented based on client interests, past travel history, and preferences. Send each group regular newsletters with tailored offers, tips, and relevant news updates.

Example: For a client who recently booked a honeymoon, you could send them a follow-up email about anniversary trip ideas or exclusive discounts on future vacations. Another campaign could focus group travel promotions for clients interested in family or group trips.

Benefit: Email marketing increases client retention and encourages repeat business. Personalized emails help build stronger relationships with clients and make them more likely to return to you for future bookings.

5. Build Partnerships with Local Businesses and Influencers

Building strategic partnerships can elevate your marketing efforts in a world where consumers value recommendations from peers and influencers.

Recommendation: Collaborate with local businesses, hotels, restaurants, and travel influencers. This approach provides mutual benefits, expanding your reach and enhancing your credibility. These partnerships can also include co-hosted events, cross-promotions, or social media shout-outs.

Example: If you specialize in adventure travel, you could partner with local outdoor gear stores to offer discounts for customers who book trips through your agency. Alternatively, collaborate with a popular travel influencer to create content about an exciting destination you offer.

Benefit: Partnering with influencers and local businesses broadens your exposure to new audiences. It can increase your social media reach, foster community connections, and add an element of credibility to your marketing efforts.

6. Offer Online Booking and Seamless Client Experience

In an age where convenience is paramount, providing a seamless online booking experience is necessary. While personalized service is essential, making the booking process efficient and easy can make the difference between a potential customer booking with you or a competitor.

Recommendation: Invest in a user-friendly website with integrated booking tools, allowing clients to research, book travel, and make down payments easily. Ensure the website is mobile-friendly, given that many clients book trips via smartphones.

Example: Offer a booking platform where clients can explore customizable vacation packages, select accommodations, and even book activities from one place. Streamlining the booking process enhances customer satisfaction and reduces the steps required to secure a sale.

Benefit: An easy-to-use website and booking platform enhance the customer experience, reduce friction, and increase conversion rates. Clients will appreciate the convenience of booking online, leading to more completed bookings and improved client satisfaction.

7. Use Paid Advertising and Retargeting

While organic marketing is important, paid advertising offers quicker access to gaining visibility and driving traffic. By strategically investing in ads, you can reach a wider audience and increase your chances of turning leads into sales.

Recommendation: Invest in Google Ads, Facebook Ads, and Instagram Ads that target your ideal clientele. Retargeting ads, in particular, can be highly effective in reminding past visitors to your website about your services, increasing the likelihood of conversion.

Example: Create a Facebook ad campaign targeting users who have previously visited your website but didn't complete a booking. You could offer a limited-time promotion for clients who book within a specific timeframe.

Benefit: Paid advertising and retargeting campaigns increase visibility and engagement with potential clients. These ads can specifically target individuals most likely to book, improving return on investment and driving more bookings. There isn't a need to completely discard existing marketing efforts. Instead, embark on a marketing makeover by refining strategies to keep up with current industry trends and consumer expectations.

The recommendations discussed (refining brand identity, leveraging social media, implementing content marketing and SEO, refining email marketing campaigns, building partnerships, offering seamless online booking, and investing in paid advertising) are important to streamlining marketing efforts for maximum profitability.

By following these recommendations, travel professionals can transform their marketing strategies to increase momentum and attract more clients. With the right combination of personalization, technology, and strategic partnerships, travel professionals can remain competitive in the ever-evolving travel industry while boosting profits and creating a loyal customer base.

Examples of How to Use Marketing Effectively as a Travel Professional. It is as Simple as 1, 2,3....and 4,5, 6!

Example #1

Use Your Brand's Message

As a travel professional specializing in eco-friendly travel, your branding should emphasize sustainable tourism and showcase partnerships with eco-conscious hotels or tours. Marketing brand messaging could include statements like "Sustainable vacations that protect the planet," highlighting how your services align with travelers' values.

Why this is successful: Refining your brand messaging will attract clients who resonate with your values and offerings. It helps position you as an authority in your niche, making gaining client trust and loyalty easier, ultimately increasing your bookings.

Example #2

Leverage Social Media

If you plan a trip to Italy for a client, share their journey on your social media platforms with beautiful photos and stories. Please encourage them to tag you in their posts and provide testimonials. Posting client experiences humanizes your brand, and storytelling captures attention more effectively than sales pitches.

Why this is successful: Social media can be a powerful tool to strengthen client relationships, increase brand visibility, and build trust. When people feel emotionally connected to your content, they are likelier to book with you and recommend your services to others.

Example #3

Optimize your website and content for SEO

If you specialize in tropical beach destinations, your website should include SEO-rich blog posts like "Top 10 Tropical Islands to Visit in 2024" or "How to Plan a Stress-Free Beach Vacation." Using SEO tools, research the most commonly searched phrases related to tropical destinations and incorporate them into your content.

Why this is successful: Optimizing your website for SEO will increase organic traffic and improve your chances of ranking higher on search engine results pages (SERPs). More visibility means more potential clients visiting your site and engaging with your content.

Example #4

Use Email to Build and Nurture Relationships

If you recently arranged a honeymoon for a couple, email them a few months later offering "Special Discounts on Anniversary Getaways" or "Romantic Weekend Retreats" tailored to their preferences. If they previously booked a European river cruise, email them when new itineraries or discounts are available.

Why this is successful: Personalized email marketing helps nurture relationships with your existing clients, keeping you at the top of their minds for future bookings. It also increases the chances of repeat business and referrals, contributing to sustained growth for your agency.

Example #5

Offering valuable content through blogs and vlogs

Consider starting a YouTube channel where you post destination walkthroughs, travel hacks, or "day-in-the-life" videos of your travel experiences. Similarly, a blog post, "7 Hidden Gems in Southeast Asia You Should Visit," can generate organic traffic and establish you as a go-to resource for expert travel advice.

Why this is successful: Providing valuable content helps establish your authority in the travel industry and keeps your audience engaged. It also drives organic traffic, which translates into increased brand visibility and higher chances of conversion.

Example #6

Expand your reach with paid advertising

You could run a Facebook ad campaign promoting a special travel deal to a specific region (e.g., a luxury beach resort) targeted at people interested in similar vacation options. Retarget users who have visited your website with a special discount code to encourage them to complete their booking.

Why this is successful: Paid advertising allows you to reach a larger, more targeted audience quickly. With retargeting, you can re-engage potential clients who have already shown interest in your services, boosting your chances of conversion and driving more sales.

Giving your travel business a marketing makeover does not require overhauling everything you've been doing. It is an opportunity to refine and enhance existing strategies to build momentum and increase profitability. By refining your brand messaging, leveraging social media, optimizing your website for SEO, and utilizing tools like email marketing, content creation, flexible booking options, and paid advertising, you strengthen your business's foundation and ensure long-term success. These recommendations offer a step toward more effective and efficient marketing efforts. They can lead your travel business to more bookings, client loyalty, and profit when implemented well. Adjusting marketing strategies helps a travel professional to thrive and grow a business in a crowded and competitive marketplace.

———————— • ————————

CHAPTER NINE

"Business opportunities are like buses,
there's always another one coming."

—RICHARD BRANSON, FOUNDER OF VIRGIN GROUP

Keep Calm and Increase Sales

As mentioned many times in earlier chapters, travel is a dynamic, ever-changing industry that has experienced some challenges in recent years. What are travel professionals to do? Keep calm, and make sales! From global pandemics to shifting consumer behaviors, travel professionals, whether in the role of travel agency owner or travel advisor (or both), have had to wade into the sea waters with a certain amount of uncertainty. Despite these challenges, there is still an immense opportunity to succeed. However, the key to unlocking that success is sales.

Every business is in business to make money. Without sales, there are no monetary resources for growth, innovation, realignment, or profit.

This chapter explores the qualities and techniques that successful entrepreneurs exhibit and then applies those same qualities and techniques to the travel business. You will see how travel professionals can implement strategies and approaches from other industries to drive success in selling travel.

A Call to Action for Travel Advisors: Calm, Confidence, Passion, and Sales Success

 Staying Calm in Uncertain Times

In the face of adversity, the most successful business owners remain calm and composed. It's a characteristic shared by top sales managers in all industries. Remaining calm not only helps you manage stress but also allows you to think clearly and make better decisions, whether in dealing with an irate client, navigating the complexities of a booking, or adapting to changing trends in travel.

During times of crisis, such as when the travel industry was hit hard by the COVID-19 pandemic, many business owners felt the pressure. However, those who could maintain their composure and stay focused on the long-term vision for their businesses found a way to come out stronger. By offering flexible booking options, communicating clearly with clients, and staying up to date with industry trends, successful travel advisors were able to build client trust and loyalty. Staying calm under pressure is a hallmark of any successful businessperson. Composure is the difference between success and failure in industries where success hinges on complex negotiations, deadlines, and expectations. It is no different in the travel industry. Travel advisors face constant pressure, client demands, fluctuating prices, and global events like natural disasters or pandemics that affect travel plans. A critical skill in overcoming these challenges is staying calm and methodical in your approach. Just as a top sales executive stays composed during a tough negotiation, a successful travel advisor approaches each situation with clarity and poise.

Staying calm allows you to think critically, assess the problem, and take appropriate actions while maintaining a positive relationship with your clients.

For instance, a travel advisor who remained calm during frequent cancellations due to uncertainty around international travel could focus on reassuring clients, keeping them informed about changing regulations and offering alternative travel options. This type of professionalism not only helps ensure repeat business but also helps establish the travel advisor as a trusted expert in the eyes of their clients.

Confidence: The Bedrock of Sales Success

Confidence is the cornerstone of any successful salesperson's strategy. As a travel advisor, you are selling experiences—memories that will last a lifetime. Your confidence in your product is crucial to communicating its value to your clients. When you are passionate about what you offer, that enthusiasm will naturally transfer to your clients.

Confidence is built on knowledge. As a travel professional, staying up to date with the latest trends in travel, learning about emerging destinations, and developing expertise in niche markets like luxury, adventure, or culinary travel will give you the foundation you need to be confident in your sales. Clients can sense when a travel advisor knows their stuff, and they will feel more comfortable trusting you with their travel plans.

It's also important to approach each interaction confidently to meet the client's needs. A confident travel advisor listens closely to clients' desires, offers tailored recommendations, and presents solutions that align with their goals. When a travel advisor exudes confidence in their ability to deliver a seamless travel experience, it also boosts the client's confidence in them. The only way to earn and maintain that trust is through confidence in your ability to deliver.

Zig Ziglar was renowned for his confidence. He always knew his products, knew how to engage customers, and understood how to inspire confidence in his clients. When you exude confidence, it's contagious. Your clients will be more inclined to trust your advice and make a purchase because they believe in your expertise and your ability to meet their needs.

For travel advisors, confidence stems from thorough knowledge. Whether knowing the best boutique hotels in Paris, understanding the most scenic routes for a European train journey, or being familiar with the ins and outs of a specific cruise line, confidence in your expertise will shine through. When you confidently speak about your product, clients feel more comfortable relying on you for their vacation planning.

Ziglar believed that people don't buy products—they buy the confidence that the salesperson has in those products. When you confidently present a travel destination or experience, your clients will not only feel like they are in safe hands, but they will also feel excited about their trip.

⭐ Passion for Your Product

Passion is contagious. When you love what you do, it shows. Passion is the driving force behind many of the best salespeople across industries, and travel is no different. Whether you specialize in cruises, wellness retreats, or cultural tours, your genuine enthusiasm for your product will speak volumes to potential clients. Passionate travel advisors are those who deeply understand the destinations they sell and who are constantly learning and exploring new products.

Take the example of a travel advisor who specializes in luxury travel. A passionate advisor could speak knowledgeably about high-end resorts, exclusive amenities, and bespoke experiences. This passion could easily be conveyed through blogs, social media posts, or one-on-one consultations. When a travel advisor is excited about a destination or experience, it's easy for clients to pick up on that energy, and they will feel more motivated to book with someone who loves what they do.

Passion is the invisible force that drives successful salespeople to go above and beyond. In the case of Zig Ziglar, his passion for sales and helping others was so genuine that it became his trademark. This passion was not just about selling but solving problems and providing value. He understood that enthusiasm will naturally inspire others when you love what you do.

For travel advisors, passion is key to building a business that clients remember and return to. You must love travel, whether it's an endless fascination with new destinations or a deep affection for a particular niche like luxury or eco-tourism. Passion will also show when you talk to clients about the experiences you sell. If you are excited about a trip to a beautiful European city, your clients will catch that excitement.

It becomes more than a job when you're passionate about your niche (i.e., adventure travel, cultural experiences, or luxury vacations). It's about sharing your enthusiasm and helping clients create unforgettable memories. This kind of passion will lead not only to more sales but also to positive referrals, repeat clients, and strong brand loyalty.

⭐ The Sales Mindset: Techniques from Other Industries

When you think of successful sales managers, what qualities come to mind? The answer often includes building relationships, solving problems, and delivering results. These are the same qualities that travel advisors need to hone to become successful salespeople.

Many techniques used by top sales executives in industries such as hospitality, retail, and even restaurants can be adapted and applied to travel. Take, for example, the techniques of Zig Ziglar, one of the most iconic salespeople of all time.

The Zig Ziglar Approach:
How Travel Professionals Can Learn
from a Sales Legend

"You don't have to be great to start, but you have to start to be great."

—Zig Ziglar

Zig Ziglar (1926-2012), an employee of WearEver Cookware, revolutionized sales and became one of the most iconic salespeople of all time. He focused on building relationships, understanding customer needs, and providing genuine value. In the case of Zig Ziglar, his passion for sales and helping others was so genuine that it became his trademark. His approach wasn't about using manipulations or tricks to close sales. He valued listening, understanding, and offering solutions that benefited the client. Ziglar's sales philosophy can be directly applied to travel. For example, his focus on relationship-building aligns perfectly with the needs of a travel professional. Travel is personal, to create experiences that fit a client's unique preferences and desires. By taking the time to understand clients' travel goals and offering them personalized solutions, a mutually beneficial lasting relationship develops that can lead to repeat business and referrals.

One of Ziglar's core principles was the importance of creating win-win situations. He believed in helping others achieve their goals, which helped him reach his own. As a travel professional, you can apply this by putting your client's needs first. For example, if a client is uncertain about their travel options, listen to their needs rather than pushing a package and guide them toward the best solution. When clients feel heard and understood, they're more likely to return and recommend your services to others.

Another key takeaway from Ziglar's approach is the power of follow-up. Ziglar understood that the sale didn't end when the deal was closed. For travel advisors, follow-up is critical. After the trip, check in with clients to see how their experience was, ask if there's anything you could improve, and ask if they would consider booking their next trip with you. This attention to detail shows your commitment to their satisfaction and creates a sense of loyalty.

Example:
Applying Zig Ziglar's Principles to Travel

Let's say you're a travel advisor specializing in luxury travel. A potential client reaches out asking for help planning a high-end European vacation. Instead of presenting a generic package, you ask thoughtful questions: What destinations are they most interested in? What types of activities do they enjoy? What's their budget? By listening carefully to their responses, you offer a curated experience that fits their unique needs.

Following the trip, you send a personalized thank-you note, asking for feedback and offering suggestions for their next trip. You also remind them of special offers, keeping the relationship strong. Through relationship-building and follow-up, you're creating not just a one-time sale but a lasting relationship with a loyal client.

The road to success in the travel industry is paved with confidence, calm, and passion.

Confidence in your product, passion for your niche, and a calm approach to challenges are all traits that will serve you well. You can meet and exceed your client's needs by using Ziglar's principles of relationship-building, listening to client's needs, and always providing value. Travel advisors who adopt these strategies will sell travel and vacation experiences that leave a lasting impact, earning client loyalty and referrals. In a world that's ever-changing, this approach will ensure that your travel business remains resilient and successful!

Food for Thought:
What Travel Professionals
Can Learn From A Highly Successful
Restaurant Sales Executive

Ira Jerome Brody, was a top sales executive in the restaurant industry, and president of Restaurant Associates, Inc., This company opened The Four Seasons restaurant in New York in 1959. Brody built his reputation by focusing on relationship-building and impeccable service. He didn't just sell meals; he sold experiences. In his role, Brody consistently demonstrated the importance of understanding the customer's needs, making personalized recommendations, and following up to ensure satisfaction. These core principles helped him turn first-time diners into regular patrons and secure high-value contracts with event planners and corporate clients.

One of Brody's key strategies was his ability to empathize with his customers. He understood that creating a memorable experience was as important as the meals served at his restaurant. By listening carefully to his client's preferences, offering tailored suggestions, and ensuring everything was executed flawlessly, Brody ensured that his customers left feeling like they had received exceptional value. This approach led to word-of-mouth referrals, repeat business and long-term client relationships.

Applying A Restaurant Sales Techniques to Travel

Travel advisors can borrow many of the same strategies that made Ira Jerome Brody successful in the restaurant industry. For example, relationship-building is at the heart of both businesses. In travel, building a relationship with your clients doesn't just end when the trip is booked. Create an ongoing connection, keep in touch with clients post-travel, and offer recommendations for future trips. In the restaurant industry, repeat business and referrals are key to long-term success.

Another strategy is the personalization of service. Travel professionals can take a page from Brody's playbook by focusing on tailored experiences. For instance, rather than simply booking a standard vacation package, a travel advisor might ask questions that help them design a unique itinerary based on the client's interests, whether a private tour of a historical site, a gourmet food tour, or a customized spa experience. Just as Ira Jerome Brody would personalize a meal for his guests, a travel advisor should personalize the travel experience.

Another key technique from the restaurant industry is follow-up. After the trip is over, a travel advisor can check in with the client to ask about their experience, ensure everything went smoothly, and address any concerns. This kind of attention to detail strengthens the client's relationship and opens the door for future bookings.

The Path to Sales Success in Travel

The travel industry, while challenging, offers immense opportunities for those who approach it with the right mindset. By remaining calm, confident, and passionate about your products and services, you can establish yourself as a trusted expert in your field. By adopting proven sales techniques from other industries, such as relationship-building, personalization, and follow-up, you can successfully improve and develop strategies to sell travel.

The example of Ira Jerome Brody, the restaurant sales executive, serves as a powerful reminder that success in sales isn't only about closing deals. It is a process of understanding your client's needs, offering tailored solutions, and creating memorable experiences. By implementing these techniques, travel advisors can build long-lasting relationships, gain loyal clients, and ultimately succeed in the competitive world of travel sales.

The road ahead may be filled with challenges, but with a steady hand, a passionate heart, and a sharp sales strategy, travel advisors can continue to navigate the ever-changing tides of the industry and emerge victorious.

———————————— • ————————————

CHAPTER TEN

*"I learned to always take on things I'd never done before.
Growth and comfort do not coexist."*

– **Ginni Rometty,** Former CEO of IBM

Sweat Equity – Investing in Your Agency's Future Success

I t can transform businesses, unlock untapped potential, and fuel the growth of your dreams. It is an investment that holds the key to your long-term success. That investment is not simply monetary but one that demands a blend of heart, soul, and sweat. I am talking about "sweat equity," the hard work, dedication, innovative thinking, and relentless drive that you, as business owners, put into your companies daily.

It doesn't matter the industry. Whether it's a small local boutique, a bustling tech startup, or a travel business, the commitment made to a company's future success matters. This chapter explores why your work is a crucial part of your business's success, how you can invest in the future, and why these investments will help you secure the future you dream of for your business. You'll be inspired to take your investment in your business to the next level. This chapter is meant to counter any doubts you may have about the importance of this investment. Are you ready to embark? This is a journey to a more successful future.

The Importance of Hard Work: a Foundation for Success

When you read "hard work," do not default to just putting in long hours or working around the clock. Hard work is a mindset dedicated to continually improving, learning, and growing. For business owners, work is the bedrock upon which everything else is built. It is the engine that drives a business forward. Without the grit, persistence, and effort put in daily, the vision, goals, and plans for the future are just ideas. They remain dormant, waiting to be awakened.

Understand that success doesn't come without effort. And it's not just the quantity of work that matters, but the quality. The businesses that thrive in today's fast-paced and competitive world combine hard work with more intelligent, strategic thinking. It's not just about doing more; it's about doing things more effectively, efficiently, and creatively.

Be resourceful. Resourcefulness requires maximizing resources, whether team members, capital, or knowledge and experience. This will require ingenuity. Every time a challenge is faced in sales, operations, or marketing, resourcefulness will help you find the solution. And when resourcefulness is combined with hard work, the business is poised to be unstoppable.

So, what does it take to ensure your business grows and becomes resilient enough to weather the challenges bound to come your way? The answer lies in how you choose to invest now in the future of your business. All industries, including travel, are entering an exciting and transformative period from 2025 to 2035. Today's decisions will determine whether your business will thrive or survive.

We are all familiar with the importance of hard work, resourcefulness, and innovation in driving a business forward. Let us look deeper at what it truly means to invest in your future business success, specifically in the context of the next decade. Although these are vital elements, this is more than a marketing or technology issue. A travel professional must understand the next decade's shifts and position a business to keep up and lead.

We live in a time when the very fabric of how people live, work, and travel is rapidly changing. The next 10+ years will bring a redefined world of business opportunities, particularly in industries like travel, where the intersection of consumer behavior, technology, and global trends will create new frontiers.

Let us outline some innovative, forward-thinking investments that can position your business to succeed, then see how they align with global and domestic trends in the travel industry. This will empower businesses to unlock potential like never before. Here are five core areas, with a special emphasis on the travel industry and how it will transform by 2035.

Why Business Investments Matter Now More Than Ever

Before discussing specifics, let's consider the bigger picture: Why will these investments matter in 2025-2035?

The business landscape is evolving. In today's world, we'll see more profound technological shifts, but the driving force behind business success will not be technology alone; human-centered innovation distinguishes leaders from loafers. We are entering an era of personalization, sustainability, wellness, and experience-first thinking.

What does that mean for business owners like you? Your investments must reflect your customers' evolving needs and desires. The demands of tomorrow's travelers are different from today's. The businesses that understand these needs and act on them will not just survive; they will thrive.

Innovative Ways to Invest in Your Business (2025-2035)

So, what are the top innovative ways businesses will need to invest in their future success over the next decade? This isn't about doing more of the same. These investments will align with the trends shaping 2025-2035 and ensure your business stays ahead of the curve.

1. Investing in Sustainability and Eco-Innovation

In the years to come, consumers will demand more from businesses regarding sustainability. This is not just a trend; it is a societal shift. By 2035, millennials and Gen Z will be the dominant demographic in consumer spending, and they are incredibly conscious of the environmental impact of their purchases.

For travel businesses, sustainability must be at the core of your offerings. Whether it's carbon offsetting services, sustainable travel options, or eco-conscious partnerships, your customers will expect you to take action to address climate change. In fact, by 2030, eco-tourism will likely become mainstream rather than the niche it is today.

The travel business can invest in things like:

Green Certifications: Partnering with eco-friendly hotels, transportation providers, and tour operators.

Carbon Offsetting Programs: Offering customers the option to offset their travel emissions.

Circular Economy Practices: Reducing waste, reusing materials, and investing in local communities to create sustainable travel experiences.

This isn't just a moral responsibility—it's a smart business decision. As more customers choose brands that align with their values, this investment will help you build trust and lasting customer loyalty.

2. Investing in Hyper-Personalization Through Data Analytics

As we approach 2025, hyper-personalization will take center stage. Consumers, especially those in the travel industry, will no longer be satisfied with generalized offerings. They will expect hyper-tailored experiences that speak directly to their interests, preferences, and values.

The question is: How do you offer personalization at scale?

This is where data analytics and AI-powered tools come in. By 2035, AI will be able to analyze large datasets to predict individual customer preferences, behavior patterns, and emotional states during their travel journey. This goes far beyond what we consider "personalized" today.

For travel business owners, here's how to invest:

Customer Data Platforms (CDPs): Invest in sophisticated tools that collect and analyze data from various customer touchpoints. This will allow you to offer customized recommendations based on past travel behavior, preferences, and real-time interactions.

AI-Powered Travel Assistants: These assistants can guide travelers before, during, and after their trips. By leveraging chatbots and machine learning, your business can provide tailored information in real-time, whether it's offering a personalized itinerary or helping them rebook flights in case of delays.

Behavioral Marketing: Use AI to craft hyper-targeted marketing campaigns that align with customers' unique travel preferences, such as their desired destinations, travel style (luxury vs. budget), and preferred travel dates.

Investing in personalization will ensure that your business doesn't just sell products—it creates memorable experiences that keep customers coming back.

3. Investing in the Future of Remote and Hybrid Work Travel

One of the most profound shifts in the past few years has been the rise of remote and hybrid work. By 2035, remote work will likely be the norm for many industries, and travel businesses must adjust to cater to the growing demand for workstations, extended stays, and bleisure (business + leisure) travel.

This trend is especially relevant to travel business owners because it opens up new opportunities for long-term stays, remote work accommodations, and the growing demand for customized work travel experiences.

How can you invest in this trend?

Remote Work Packages: Offer tailored packages for professionals who want to work while traveling. These packages could include accommodations with high-speed internet, flexible workspaces, and long-term stay options.

Digital Nomad Networks: Invest in partnerships or networks that help digital nomads connect with local experiences and resources. These include co-working spaces, local experiences, or even a concierge service to help them find the best locations to work from.

Wellness-Focused Travel: With the rise of remote work, there's also a greater demand for wellness tourism. Combining work and wellness retreats, offering yoga, meditation, and self-care options, will appeal to those who want to recharge while staying productive.

This investment taps into a growing market and positions your business as forward-thinking and aligned with the changing way people work and travel.

4. Investing in Virtual and Augmented Reality Experiences

By 2035, virtual reality (VR) and augmented reality (AR) will completely redefine how travelers experience destinations and activities before stepping on a plane. Imagine allowing your customers to virtually tour a destination, hotel, or local attraction before booking. For your travel business, VR and AR will offer immersive marketing tools, pre-trip experiences, and innovative ways to experience travel from home.

Investing in VR/AR technology means:

Virtual Previews: Create immersive, interactive experiences that allow customers to explore destinations, hotels, and activities in 360° before making decisions.

Enhanced Travel Planning: Use VR/AR to help customers virtually experience accommodations, destinations, and even day trips to better plan their trips.

Brand Differentiation: Providing innovative experiences such as virtual tours or AR-guided city tours will set your business apart from the competition.

5. Investing in Emotional Intelligence and Service Excellence

The customers of 2025-2035 will expect excellent service and emotional intelligence from the brands they interact with. They will seek businesses that understand their emotional journey, especially in the travel industry, where experiences are deeply personal. Whether they're seeking relaxation, adventure, or connection, how your business makes them feel will be a decisive factor in their loyalty.

Here's how to invest in service excellence:

Training Programs in Emotional Intelligence (EI): Equip your staff with the skills to recognize and respond to customers' emotional needs. Travel experiences are deeply tied to emotions, and the ability to connect with clients on this level will differentiate your business.

Empathetic Customer Service: Build customer service protocols beyond solving issues and focusing on understanding and alleviating your travelers' concerns or anxieties. This can make all the difference in turning a one-time traveler into a loyal customer.

As travel professionals, the next decade is your opportunity to redefine future success. It's a chance to invest to ensure your business thrives, grows, and adapts to the rapidly changing landscape.

Sustainability, personalization, remote work travel, immersive technology, and emotional intelligence are not just trends. They are the foundation of the future. Investing in these areas will position your business for future success.

The journey ahead is one of tremendous opportunity, and by investing in innovative ways to meet the needs of tomorrow's travelers, you'll be ready to lead the way in a changing world.

 Top Five Ways to Invest in Your Business Future Success

Now, let's talk about the top five ways to invest in the future of your business. Each strategy is a pillar on which you will build your company's future. Focusing on these will result in a substantial profit return and long-term sustainability.

1. Invest in Your People

Your team is your greatest asset. As business owners, it's easy to get caught up in the day-to-day operations and overlook the most critical element—the people who make your vision a reality. Investing in your employees, hiring the right talent, and fostering an environment where they can grow is one of the most valuable investments you can make.

Training, encouraging development, and creating a positive company culture will improve morale, productivity, and loyalty. This also helps you retain top talent, saving time and money spent on recruitment and turnover. Remember, when your team thrives, your business thrives.

2. Invest in Technology and Innovation

Technology has transformed every industry. As a business owner, staying ahead of the technological curve is not a luxury; it's a necessity. Whether you invest in better customer management systems, upgrade your website, or adopt tools that streamline operations, technology is one of the most powerful ways to scale your business.

However, success is not having the latest gadgets or software. It will result from leveraging technology to innovate and provide unique value to your customers. Whether through automation, data analytics, or new product development, technology allows you to make smarter decisions faster.

3. Invest in Marketing and Brand Building

Your brand is your reputation. The way customers perceive your business can make or break your success. Invest in marketing strategies that build your brand, attract new customers, and retain your existing ones. A strong marketing plan will help you increase visibility, differentiate yourself from the competition, and create customer loyalty.

Marketing is an investment—not a cost. Whether you focus on digital marketing, social media, content creation, or traditional advertising, consistent investment in marketing can give you a high return in the form of leads, conversions, and growth.

4. Invest in Customer Experience

Great businesses are built around exceptional customer experiences. As customers become more discerning, companies must constantly evolve to meet their needs. Invest in providing an experience that exceeds expectations through better customer service, a smoother purchasing process, or personalized offerings.

Customer satisfaction is an investment in brand loyalty. Happy customers become repeat buyers and brand advocates. They'll refer others to your business, and their positive reviews will bring you credibility and new opportunities.

5. Invest in Financial Health and Planning

Financial health is the backbone of your business. Even if everything else is in place, your business can falter without solid financial planning and proper cash flow management. Invest in sound financial practices, including budgeting, forecasting, and setting up strong financial reporting systems. Hiring an accountant or financial expert to guide you through decisions is wise.

Good financial management ensures that your business has the resources to weather difficult times, make strategic investments, and expand when the opportunity arises.

 Ways Travel Business Owners Can Invest in Their Future Success

Now that we've covered the general principles of business investment let's dive into the specifics of the travel industry. The travel industry, in particular, has faced unprecedented challenges in recent years, but it has also emerged with new opportunities. As a travel business owner, investing in your future success means staying agile and adapting to new market realities. Here are three crucial ways to invest in your travel business's future.

1. Invest in Digital Marketing and Online Presence

The travel industry has become increasingly digital. More customers are researching and booking travel online than ever before. In this highly competitive space, having a robust online presence is essential. This includes having an engaging website, a strong social media presence, and using digital marketing strategies to target potential customers where they spend their time.

An effective digital marketing plan for your travel business can include content marketing (like blogs or destination guides), social media campaigns, influencer partnerships, email marketing, and search engine optimization (SEO). The goal is to ensure that your business appears at the top of the search results when potential customers seek travel experiences. If you can effectively capture the attention of your target market, your bookings will soar.

2. Invest in Customer Relationship Management (CRM) Systems

The travel industry thrives on relationships. Whether you're selling package tours, hotel bookings, or destination experiences, keeping track of your customers and their preferences is crucial. A CRM system helps you manage customer data, keep track of past bookings, and send personalized offers.

This investment enables you to provide a more tailored experience for each customer, which is invaluable in a service-based industry like travel. The ability to communicate personalized promotions, offer loyalty rewards and follow up with clients post-trip increases customer retention and builds long-term relationships, ultimately driving repeat business.

3. Invest in Employee Training and Specialization

In the travel industry, the personal touch is often the difference between gaining a client's trust and losing them to a competitor. By investing in specialized training for your staff (training on specific destinations, customer service excellence, or the latest trends in travel), you ensure that your team can provide the best possible experience to your customers.

Additionally, specialized knowledge in specific travel sectors, such as luxury, adventure tours, or corporate travel, can differentiate your business. Customers want experts who understand their needs and offer tailored recommendations. This level of service and expertise will elevate your reputation and drive customer loyalty.

Dispelling Doubts:
Why These Investments Are Worth It

Some may think, "But isn't investing in my business risky? What if I don't see a return?" The risks of not investing in your business are far greater than those of doing so.

The world is changing rapidly. Competition is intensifying. Consumer expectations are higher than ever. If you don't continuously improve and invest in your business's future, your competitors will. You'll find yourself stuck in a cycle of stagnation while others grow, innovate, and lead the way.

Every investment you make (in people, technology, marketing, customer experience, or finances) is an investment in the growth and sustainability of your business. Yes, there will be risks. But the greatest risk is failing to take action, move forward, and create a vision that transcends the immediate moment.

The travel industry's demand for personalized, expert, and innovative experiences is growing. By investing wisely, you will position your business to survive and thrive.

As business owners, the most important thing you can do for your company's future is invest in it now. Your sweat equity and the right strategic investments will ensure your business continues growing, adapting, and succeeding for years.

Whether you focus on digital marketing, customer experience, or employee training, every investment is a step toward securing a brighter, more prosperous future. Never underestimate the power of hard work, strategic planning, and innovation. Your business's future is in your hands, and by making these investments, you'll create a lasting legacy.

———————— • ————————

"The only thing that matters is the work you put in and the passion you bring to the table."

—GARY VAYNERCHUK,
AUTHOR, INVESTOR, SPEAKER, AND SOCIAL MEDIA INFLUENCER

The Big Comeback – a Mindset Shift

The Power of a Mindset Shift: How Travel Professionals Can Overcome Setbacks and Reclaim Success

In today's rapidly changing business landscape, many entrepreneurs and business owners grapple with the consequences of past failures, market downturns, and an overwhelming sense of uncertainty. However, as any successful leader or business professional knows, it is not the setbacks that define the company but the response to those setbacks. To return to a path of success, travel professionals must embrace the transformative power of shifting their mindset from defeat to empowerment. Focus not on the weight of their past mistakes but on the lessons they've learned and the opportunities they now see.

Say hello to a mindset shift.

A mindset shift from dwelling on past failures to thinking progressively and with the resilience of a champion is arguably the most critical factor in turning around a business. Success can be found in many aspects of business: operations, strategy, marketing, leadership, and even the way entrepreneurs approach their own personal growth. But no matter the area, the foundation for achieving it is a mentality that rejects stagnation and embraces growth, adaptability, and innovation.

Travel Professionals Can Embrace Resilience: Lessons from Athletes

The journey to success is never linear, and setbacks are part of the process. Famous athletes who have endured monumental challenges on their way to victory provide valuable lessons in persistence and resilience. Two athletes stand out as paragons of how a mindset shift can transform failure into triumph.

Michael Jordan:
The Pursuit of Excellence

No athlete is more emblematic of overcoming failure and becoming a champion than Michael Jordan. Widely regarded as one of the greatest basketball players of all time, Jordan's career is a testament to the power of perseverance and the refusal to allow failure to dictate his future.

Early in his career, Jordan faced a significant setback. He was cut from his high school basketball team, a moment that could have ended his dream before it even started. Instead of succumbing to the sting of rejection, Jordan used it as fuel to drive himself to improve. "I've missed more than 9,000 shots in my career. I've lost almost 300 games. 26 times I've been trusted to take the game-winning shot and missed. I've failed over and over and over again in my life. And that is why I succeed," he famously said.

Jordan's ability to embrace failure and view it as a stepping stone to greatness is a mindset that business owners can emulate. In the world of business, setbacks and failures are inevitable, but they do not define the end of the journey. Like Jordan, entrepreneurs must use each failure as a lesson and opportunity to refine their skills, recalibrate their approach, and push themselves closer to success.

Serena Williams: Overcoming Adversity

Serena Williams, wife, mother of two, entrepreneur, fashion icon, and, of course, the Greatest Of All Time (GOAT) in the world of sports, faced numerous challenges throughout her career, including physical injuries, personal struggles, and the pressure of being one of the most successful tennis players in history. Yet, Williams has always been known for her resilience and ability to rise after setbacks.

In 2018, after undergoing surgery for a pulmonary embolism and battling postpartum complications, Williams was faced with the daunting task of returning to top-level tennis. Despite her hardships, she returned to the court with unwavering determination. "I don't like to lose – at anything – yet I've learned that losing is part of life," Williams once said. "It's how you learn from your losses that will make you a champion."

Williams' ability to continue pushing forward despite personal and professional setbacks is a powerful reminder that business owners, too, must be willing to face adversity with strength and a mindset focused on long-term success. The journey to business success is not without obstacles, but those obstacles can be overcome with the right mindset.

Business Leaders Who Didn't Let Failure Define Them

Many entrepreneurs have faced financial ruin, crippling doubts, and countless rejections. However, their success stories are proof that the key to success is not avoiding failure but learning how to rise from it.

Thomas Edison: The Pursuit of Innovation

Thomas Edison, one of the most prolific inventors in history, is another business leader who succeeded because he refused to allow failure to define him. Edison's most famous invention, the light bulb, was the product of thousands of failed experiments. In fact, Edison himself stated, "I have not failed. I've just found 10,000 ways that won't work."

Edison's mindset was one of experimentation and persistence. His ability to reframe failure as part of the innovation process led to one of the most significant technological advancements in history. Business owners can learn from Edison's example by viewing each setback as an opportunity for improvement rather than a permanent failure.

Steve Jobs: The Resilient Visionary

Steve Jobs, co-founder of Apple, exemplified the power of a resilient mindset. In 1985, Jobs was ousted from Apple, the very company he founded. Many would have given up after such a public and personal setback. Instead, Jobs viewed the experience as an opportunity to grow. "Remembering that you are going to die is the best way I know to avoid the trap of thinking you have something to lose. You are already naked. There is no reason not to follow your heart," he once said.

Jobs went on to found NeXT and acquire Pixar, which eventually led him back to Apple, where he oversaw the development of the iPod, iPhone, and iPad—products that revolutionized the tech industry. Jobs' story reminds us that setbacks and failures do not mark the end of a business career but can instead be the beginning of a new chapter filled with possibilities for growth and reinvention.

Shifting Your Mindset to Yield Success As A Travel Professional

If a mindset shift is the most important part of returning to success, how can travel professionals cultivate such a shift in their lives? Here are five strategies for changing one's mindset from defeat to empowerment:

1. Embrace Failure as a Learning Opportunity

As exemplified by the stories of Michael Jordan, Serena Williams, Thomas Edison, and Steve Jobs, failure is an inevitable part of success. Rather than fearing failure, travel professionals should embrace it as a learning opportunity. Each mistake provides valuable lessons that can inform better decision-making in the future.

2. Focus on Progress, Not Perfection

One of the greatest challenges for business owners is the desire for perfection. However, perfection is often unattainable, and striving for it can cause unnecessary stress and burnout. Instead, focus on making incremental progress. Every small step forward is a victory that can eventually lead to larger successes.

3. Visualize Success

Visualization is a powerful tool used by successful athletes, entrepreneurs, and leaders. By picturing your goals and the steps necessary to achieve them, you prime your mind for success. Take time each day to visualize your desired outcomes, whether a successful product launch, a growing customer base, or achieving a revenue goal.

4. Cultivate a Growth Mindset

A growth mindset, the belief that abilities and intelligence can be developed through hard work and dedication, is crucial for overcoming challenges. Rather than viewing challenges as insurmountable obstacles, a growth mindset allows you to see them as opportunities to learn and grow.

5. Surround Yourself with Positivity

The people you surround yourself with can significantly impact your mindset. Seek out mentors, peers, and employees who are positive, supportive, and solution-oriented. Having a network of individuals who uplift you can help foster a mindset of confidence and resilience.

Success in business is not just about executing the right strategy or having the best product. It is also about developing the mental fortitude to keep pushing forward, even in the face of adversity. Business owners who shift their mindset from focusing on past failures to thinking like champions—who embrace setbacks as part of their journey—can unlock new opportunities for growth and success. The stories of athletes like Michael Jordan and Serena Williams and business legends like Thomas Edison and Steve Jobs prove that failure is not an endpoint but a stepping stone toward greater achievements.

By adopting a mindset that focuses on growth, learning, and perseverance, business owners can set themselves on a path to success—one that is not defined by their failures but by their ability to rise above them and keep moving forward with purpose and confidence.

No different are the business owners and professionals in the travel industry. Travel professionals prioritize progress, innovation, and resilience over dwelling on past mistakes like their counterparts in any other field. The journey back to success is paved through various facets, often through enhancing customer experiences, refining operational strategies, or innovating with new technologies. Yet, at the core of it all is a mindset shift: moving away from focusing on past failures and shifting to a champion's mentality—one that is forward-thinking and ready to embrace new possibilities.

Overcoming Setbacks in Travel: Lessons from Industry Leaders

The travel industry has had its fair share of challenges over the years. From the economic crash of 2008 to the global disruption caused by the COVID-19 pandemic, travel businesses have had to adapt in ways that test their resilience. Here are two examples of travel industry giants who demonstrated unwavering resolve in the face of adversity, turning failure into success by shifting their mindset.

Richard Branson and Virgin Holidays: Resilience in the Face of Setbacks

Richard Branson, founder of Virgin Group, is a prime example of an entrepreneur whose ability to recover from failure has helped him build an empire in the travel and leisure industry, including the successful Virgin Holidays business. Branson is no stranger to setbacks, especially when launching new ventures.

One of Branson's early business failures was Virgin Cola (never heard of it, right?), which failed to compete with established brands like Coca-Cola and Pepsi. Despite this, Branson's resilience and ability to learn from his mistakes propelled him forward. In his book Losing My Virginity, Branson shares a pivotal piece of advice: "You don't learn to walk by following rules. You learn by doing, and by falling over." His ability to embrace failure, learn from it, and use those lessons to propel Virgin Holidays into success is a testament to the importance of mindset in business recovery.

Branson's success in the travel industry, including Virgin Holidays, illustrates how critical it is for travel business owners to adapt and innovate rather than be paralyzed by past failures. Branson turned Virgin Holidays into one of the most recognized travel brands globally by focusing on creating a customer-focused experience and maintaining a sense of adventure and risk-taking.

Glenn Fogel and Booking.com: Building Resilience After the Pandemic

Glenn Fogel, CEO of Booking Holdings (the parent company of Booking.com), faced one of the toughest challenges in the travel sector when the COVID-19 pandemic caused travel to plummet, leading to billions in losses. But rather than giving up, Fogel doubled down on his company's long-term vision and focused on rebuilding.

Fogel has always advocated for thinking long-term, even in the face of adversity. In an interview with Harvard Business Review, Fogel shared, "It's all about mindset: we focused on the future, not the current challenges, and realized that recovery would happen, but we needed to keep investing in technology and innovations to be ready for the shift when it came."

Under his leadership, Booking.com has survived the pandemic and thrived in its aftermath by embracing digital transformation, enhancing its platform's functionality, and investing in customer-centric experiences. Fogel's ability to stay forward-focused and optimistic through the pandemic shows how important mindset is in overcoming industry-specific challenges.

Famous Travel Business Leaders: Overcoming Adversity and Pushing Forward

The stories of Branson and Fogel show that, even in the most challenging times, a mindset shift can lead to breakthroughs and success. This principle is also true for other well-known travel business owners who embraced perseverance, innovation, and a forward-thinking attitude to secure their place in the industry.

Walt Disney and Disneyland: Visionary Leadership

Walt Disney's vision for Disneyland was initially met with skepticism, with many believing the concept of a theme park based on movies would fail. When he pitched the idea for Disneyland, Disney faced rejection from potential investors who doubted the feasibility of such an expensive venture. However, rather than dwelling on these failures, Disney remained focused on his vision, famously stating, "All our dreams can come true, if we have the courage to pursue them."

When Disneyland opened in 1955, it was not the flawless launch many had hoped for. The park suffered from operational mishaps, including overcrowding, unfinished attractions, and a heat wave that frustrated guests. Yet, Disney's unshakable belief in his idea led to the park's expansion and enduring success. His ability to persevere through these early challenges, and his mindset that no setback was too great—was key to establishing Disneyland as a global icon.

Brian Chesky and Airbnb: Reinventing the Travel Model

Brian Chesky, the co-founder of Airbnb, is another entrepreneur who exemplifies resilience in the face of failure. When Chesky and his co-founders launched Airbnb in 2008, their concept of renting out spare rooms to travelers was met with significant resistance. Many doubted whether people would ever trust strangers with their homes, and the company faced financial struggles in its early years.

During the 2008 financial crisis, Airbnb struggled to gain traction, and the founders were forced to take drastic measures to keep the business afloat.

Despite the challenges, Chesky's mindset never wavered. "If we're going to fail, we're going to fail big," he said. "But we're going to keep going. We're going to keep pushing forward." That determination paid off, as Airbnb eventually became a hospitality and travel industry leader. The company's ability to evolve with market trends, embrace innovation, and adapt to customer needs, all while keeping a progressive mindset, allowed it to thrive and grow during difficult times.

Shifting Your Mindset to Achieve Business Success

These examples demonstrate that the path to success is rarely free of obstacles. The ability to overcome setbacks often separates successful business leaders from those who give up in the face of adversity. So, how can travel professionals and travel business owners adopt the mindset necessary to achieve success? Here are some practical ways:

1. Reframe Failure

As Richard Branson and Brian Chesky have shown, failure is not the end—it's simply part of the journey. Business owners can learn more from their mistakes than from their successes. Each failure holds a lesson that can improve their approach to future challenges. By embracing failure as part of the process, they can reduce their fear of taking risks and open themselves up to innovation and growth.

2. Seek Challenges

A growth mindset, advocated by Walt Disney and Glenn Fogel, encourages business owners to see challenges as opportunities for development rather than obstacles to avoid. This mindset involves understanding that intelligence and abilities can be developed through dedication and hard work. Focus on learning new skills, improving your operations, and refining your strategies to build your business.

3. Invest in Innovation

Innovation is key to staying competitive in the travel industry. Whether adopting new technology, improving customer service, or exploring new travel trends, business owners should always look for ways to enhance their offerings. Branson and Fogel were committed to innovation, ensuring their businesses evolved with the times.

4. Focus on the Long-Term Vision

Brian Chesky's focus on Airbnb's long-term vision, even when the company faced near collapse, is a great reminder that setbacks are often temporary. Stay focused on the bigger picture, and don't let short-term struggles derail your vision. Long-term success is achievable with patience, persistence, and a clear focus.

5. Build Supportive Networks

Just as Richard Branson and Walt Disney had strong teams and supporters behind them, business owners must surround themselves with positive, like-minded individuals who encourage and help navigate tough times. Seek mentors, partners, and employees who believe in your vision and can help you overcome the inevitable challenges. By focusing on long-term goals, embracing innovation, and cultivating a mindset that thrives in the face of adversity, travel business owners and travel professionals can rise above their setbacks and lead their companies to new heights.

As Walt Disney said, *"The way to get started is to quit talking and begin doing."*

Notes for the Journey Ahead

———————•———————

"Knowing is not enough. We must apply.
Willing is not enough. We must do."

—BRUCE LEE, LEGENDARY FILM ACTOR.

He was correct. Gaining knowledge or learning something without applying it is a waste of time, rendering the knowledge useless.

As you come to the end of this insightful book, take time to reflect on what you have learned and how it can be applied to achieve greater success. The information in this book is exciting and offers motivation, strategies, and a path forward to success with a renewed mindset. Many successful entrepreneurs, highly effective marketing managers, and business leaders in many different industries use these strategies.

But here's the key: just knowing about these strategies isn't enough. Knowledge on its own is just information. Only through action, consistency, and real effort can you turn that knowledge into results. Yes, you are passionate about your business. You care and take your success seriously. Yes, you are dedicated to offering outstanding travel experiences and building strong relationships with your clients. But no matter how great your passion, passion alone doesn't guarantee success.

What's required is a roadmap to success, which is a clear, strategic plan that you can follow. A roadmap that takes the insights discussed here and puts them into action. This is where focus is needed. It's simple, it really is. But simplicity doesn't mean easy. The strategies covered are straightforward but require effort, persistence, and consistency. It's easy to get excited about a new idea or strategy, but maintaining the discipline to stay committed to it over time sets the successful person apart from those who struggle.

Think about it: how many times have you learned something that you thought could change your business, only to let it fade into the background as you got caught up in daily operations? We've all been there. It's human nature. But I urge you to do something different this time.

As you finish reading this book and return to your business, commit to reviewing this information regularly. Revisit these strategies when you feel your momentum starting to slow down. As is often quoted, "Remember your "why." Remember why you are in the travel industry and own your own business.

That's the key. Momentum. It can be fleeting and losing it in the hustle and bustle of running a business is easy. But if you make it a habit to reread this book and revisit these strategies, you'll have a strong foundation to reignite your energy and push forward. You'll see results when you can consistently apply these strategies. And those results will fuel even greater success. You have what it takes. Now, get to it!

Victoria Henley is an MBA, CTA, VTA, and member of the American Society of Travel Advisors (ASTA), Cruise Lines International Association (CLIA), and International Airlines Travel Agent Network (IATAN). She has over 20 years of experience working in the marketing departments for international corporations (Nike), media companies (Houston Chronicle-Hearst), professional organizations (American Nurses Association), and nonprofits (Sports in Education Charitable Foundation). She is the founder of Joyage Travel Services LLC, and the visionary and creator of Revive & Thrive Getaways and Retreats®, her trademarked group travel business specializing in curated experiences designed to help individuals escape the daily grind and return refreshed, inspired, and ready to thrive. Holding certifications in several travel specialties, Victoria blends her award-winning creative marketing strategies with travel industry knowledge to deliver valuable insights that drive success for travel professionals. With a comprehensive understanding of marketing, she provides a unique perspective that empowers travel professionals to excel in today's competitive market. Victoria earned her Bachelor of Science in Marketing from Southern University and A&M College in Baton Rouge, Louisiana, and a Master of Business Administration in Management from Texas Southern University in Houston, Texas.

Visit www.JTravelServices.com/advisor for more information, to sign up for travel marketing insights, to schedule an appointment for consultation, and to register for upcoming events and webinars.

Jet Setter Jottings & Wander Notes

REFERENCES

Chapter 5

Booking.com. 2023. Sustainability Trends in Travel. Retrieved from https://www.booking.com

Intrepid Travel. (2023). Sustainable Travel. Retrieved from https://www.intrepidtravel.com

McKinsey & Company. 2022. The Future of Travel: Personalization at Scale. Retrieved from https://www.mckinsey.com

U.S. Travel Association. (2022). Travel Trends: The Shift Toward Experience-Driven Travel. Retrieved from https://www.ustravel.org

Expedia Group. 2023. Expedia Technology and Personalization. Retrieved from https://www.expediagroup.com

Airbnb. 2023. Airbnb Experiences: Redefining Travel. Retrieved from https://www.airbnb.com

Captivating Travel Market Report: Unveiling The Secrets Of The Industry – World News Now. https://ieripolikq.info/2024/05/22/travel-market-report/

Chapter 10

6 Digital Marketing Trends for 2025 | Z Omni Serve. https://www.
zomniserve.com/digital-marketing/6-digital-marketing-trends-
for-2025/)

Source: Navigating The Challenges Of Marketing In A Cookieless Future -
Cybertek Marketing. https://cybertekmarketing.com/digital-marketing/
navigating-the-challenges-of-marketing-in-a-cookieless-future-2/)

Chapter 11

Learning Little from Victory, Much More from Defeat: A Motivational
Journey. https://myhabits.info/news/learning-little-from-
victory-much-more-from-defeat-a-motivational-journey; Ruiz,
Matthew D. "A Psychotheology of Losing." (2017). https://doi.
org/10.7290/jcskls04685j.

11 Famous Failures that will Inspire You to Succeed. https://inspidose.
com/visualstories/11famous-failures-that-will-inspire-you-
to-succeed

The Resilient Path to Greatness: Fighters and Entrepreneurs" – Huewave
Media. https://huewavemedia.com/2023/09/20/the-resilient-path-
to-greatness-fighters-and-entrepreneurs/; Breakthrough Now and
Live Your Best LifeRockstar Spirit. https://www.rockstarspirit.
com/post/breakthrough-now-and-live-your-best-life; Dream Big
and Dare to Fail: The Pathway to Achieving Greatness. https://
sajeevdev.com/dream-big-and-dare-to-fail-the-pathway-to-
achieving-greatness/

www.ingramcontent.com/pod-product-compliance
Lightning Source LLC
Chambersburg PA
CBHW071547120626
46550CB00006B/2620